THE POWER OF STORIES

How Emotional Intelligence in the Bible Can Help You Navigate Life's Challenges

PAMELA BUCY PIERSON
CATHERINE JOHNSON RANDALL

CSS Publishing Company, Inc.
Lima, Ohio

THE POWER OF STORIES

FIRST EDITION
Copyright © 2024
by CSS Publishing Co., Inc.

Published by CSS Publishing Company, Inc., Lima, Ohio 45807. All rights reserved. No part of this publication may be reproduced in any manner whatsoever without the prior permission of the publisher, except in the case of brief quotations embodied in critical articles and reviews. Inquiries should be addressed to: CSS Publishing Company, Inc., Permissions Department, 5450 N. Dixie Highway, Lima, Ohio 45807.

Library of Congress Cataloging-in-Publication Data

Names: Pierson, Pamela Bucy, 1953- author. | Randall, Catherine J. (Catherine Johnson), author.
Title: The power of stories : emotional intelligence in the Bible / by Pamela Bucy Pierson and Catherine J. Randall.
Description: [Lima, Ohio] : [CSS Publishing Company, Inc.], [2024]
Identifiers: LCCN 2024014835 (print) | LCCN 2024014836 (ebook) | ISBN 9780788031076 (paperback) | ISBN 9780788031083 (adobe pdf)
Subjects: LCSH: Emotions--Biblical teaching. | Emotional intelligence--Biblical teaching. | Bible stories.
Classification: LCC BS680.E4 P54 2024 (print) | LCC BS680.E4 (ebook) | DDC 204/.4--dc23/eng/20240826
LC record available at https://lccn.loc.gov/2024014835
LC ebook record available at https://lccn.loc.gov/2024014836

For more information about CSS Publishing Company resources, visit our website at www.csspub.com, email us at csr@csspub.com, or call (800) 241-4056.

e-book:
ISBN-13: 978-0-7880-3108-3
ISBN-10: 0-7880-3108-2

ISBN-13: 978-0-7880-3107-6
ISBN-10: 0-7880-3107-4   PRINTED IN USA

CONTENTS

ACKNOWLEDGMENTS 5

CHAPTER ONE: INTRODUCTION 7

CHAPTER TWO: MANAGING STRESS 18

CHAPTER THREE: DEALING WITH NEGATIVE EMOTIONS 30

CHAPTER FOUR: RESILIENCE 41

CHAPTER FIVE: EMOTIONAL STABILITY:
MANAGING OUR EMOTIONAL TEMPERAMENT 56

CHAPTER SIX: HABITS 66

CHAPTER SEVEN: SELF-REGULATION 78

CHAPTER EIGHT: SELF-AWARENESS 87

CHAPTER NINE: FORGIVENESS 95

CHAPTER TEN: EMPATHY 103

CHAPTER ELEVEN: STRENGTHS AND WEAKNESSES,
KNOWING WHAT THEY ARE AND HOW TO MANAGE THEM 113

CHAPTER TWELVE: ADAPTABILITY 121

CHAPTER THIRTEEN: GRATITUDE 132

CHAPTER FOURTEEN: CONCLUSION 142

APPENDIX A: LECTIO DIVINA AS A MEDITATION PRACTICE
FOR THE LESSONS OF THIS BOOK 153

APPENDIX B: MINDFULNESS MEDITATION 155

ENDNOTES 158

ACKNOWLEDGMENTS

We are immensely grateful to the eleven people who have shared their journeys in life with us: Tammy Bradford, John Dorsey, Andrea Edmonds, Kathy Hayes, Ray Hinton, Liz Huntley, Demarcus Joiner, Barry Mason, Betty Shirley, Alyce Spruell, and Bryan Stevenson. We are honored to donate the proceeds from this book to nonprofits associated with them.

We thank the dozens of friends and family who have read, workshopped, and critiqued drafts of this book, including Jan Brakefield, Julie Bucy, Reverend Scott Clark, Bryan Fair, Reverend Dr. Michael Foster, Kay Gillette, Reverend Dr. David Greenhaw, Kathy Echols, Reverend Genie Gamble, Gina Johnson, Nancy Jones, Peggy Kelly, Vera Key, The Reverend Dr. Russell Levenson, Jr., Carolyn Mason, Dr. Rebecca Matteo, Jacqueline Morgan, John Oneal, Jan Orr-Harter, Bobby Prince, Dena Prince, The Reverend Deacon Cindy Roff, Ryan Stallings, Bishop B. Michael Watson, Abbie Woodson, and Sister Wright.

We give special thanks to our friend Dr. Rebecca Matteo who provided Appendix B. These wise and kind friends have enriched our lives and this book.

We also thank the many friends, acquaintances, and family who have shared their thoughts and questions. We give a special thanks to our dear friend Kathy Hayes, whom you will meet in Chapter Three. Kathy breathed life into this book when it needed it and unceasingly brings heart and love to us.

CHAPTER ONE: INTRODUCTION

The Bible is a book of faith. It is also about the challenges and opportunities of life — those that bring us to our knees but also teach us strength and courage. Above all, the Bible is a book of stories: stories of people just like us who experience despair, joy, fear, purpose, sadness, kindness, love, and faith.

The stories in this book are about individuals of the Bible: men and women, young and old, wealthy and poor. They are from the Old and New Testaments. They are the esteemed of society and the shunned. Other stories are about modern-day individuals: black and white, male and female, ranging in age from twenty to 94. One individual was a teenage mother. Another grew up in government housing. Two attended segregated schools. One suffered from child sexual abuse. Another survived cancer. One individual served almost thirty years on death row before being released by appellate courts. Like the people of the Bible, these modern-day individuals are from all walks of life.

This book is also about emotional intelligence, a relatively new field of behavioral science made possible by new technologies. Interest by the general public in emotional intelligence has exploded in recent years. Books, courses, podcasts, and social media have proliferated. Fields as diverse as business, the armed services, health care, education, and law have responded with training and resources. Surprisingly, there are few books linking emotional intelligence with faith, spirituality, or religion. Our book does so.

We draw upon the rich trove of behavioral science on emotional intelligence to highlight some of the fascinating and important insights from it. We use these insights and the stories herein to explain emotional intelligence in an approachable and accessible way to show how emotional intelligence applies in daily life. We see individuals using emotional intelligence (or sometimes, not). We see people grow in their emotional intelligence. We see how emotional intelligence helps them and can help us to be happier, more resilient, and less stressed, as well as live more fully into the image of God.

Whether one views the Bible as literal or sacred truth, its wisdom can be life changing. The stories in this book show how the field of behavioral science, specifically emotional intelligence, like the disciplines of history, anthropology, biology, and archeology, can help us see the wisdom of the Bible from a new perspective that enriches our day-to-day lives as well as our spiritual journeys.

What is Emotional Intelligence?

Simply stated, emotional intelligence is the ability to understand and manage one's emotions. It is a set of skills to help us prevent distressing emotions from overwhelming us and to nurture positive emotions like resilience, self-awareness, empathy, and gratitude. As the studies discussed in this book show, "EQ" is proving more determinative than IQ in life satisfaction and life success in almost every way; it is fundamental to a life of happiness and contentment:

> "Much evidence testifies that people who are emotionally adept, who know and manage their own feelings well, and who read and deal effectively with other people's feelings, are at an advantage in any domain of life, whether romance and intimate relationships or picking up the unspoken rules that govern success in organizational politics. People with well-developed emotional skills are also more likely to be content and effective in their lives, mastering the habits of mind that foster their own productivity; people who cannot marshal some control over their emotional life fight inner battles that sabotage their ability to focus on work and clear thought."[1]

Emotional intelligence, of course, has been around for a long time, but seeing it as a discipline is "new" because the tools to research and study it did not exist until the late twentieth century. One such tool, fMRI (functional Magnetic Resonance Imaging) which became available in the 1970s, allows scientists to study brain activity in "real time" as individuals actually experience emotions, and as emotions change. Also beginning in the 1970s and accelerating since with computer-driven analytics, scientists now have tools to amass large data sets, making it possible to study and compare individuals over time, even years, to see how emotions impact long-term human physical health and wellbeing. With the advent of these tools, the field of behavioral science changed significantly. Before them, the study of human behavior was dependent on what could be learned from talking with individuals and observing their behaviors visually. This confined behavioral science primarily to the study of psychological disorders: seeking to understand and describe disorders and help those with them. Now, however, because of fMRIs and the availability of longitudinal studies of large data sets, behavioral science has broadened beyond the study of psychological disorders to include the study of life strategies of those who function well in life. This has become the field of emotional intelligence: what the skills of emotional intelligence are, how to build and strengthen them, and why they are important.

A well-known study in the 1960s of four-year-olds and marshmallows is a classic in emotional intelligence. Focusing on the EQ skills of willpower and ability to defer gratification, researchers studied four-year-old children (who were in preschool at Stanford University). A researcher placed a four-year-old child in a room with a one-way mirror, then put a marshmallow on the table in front of the child with instructions that if the child could wait to eat the marshmallow until the researcher returned, the child could have two marshmallows. The researcher left the room and went to an adjoining room to observe the child through a one-way mirror. About one-third of the children were able to resist eating the marshmallow until the researcher returned. If you have a few minutes, watch a video of this study.[2] The children's strategies for resisting the marshmallow (or not) are fascinating, and often hilarious.

The researchers followed the four-year-olds into adulthood and found dramatic differences between the children who had resisted the marshmallow and the children who had not. The "resisters," as adults, were more positive, self-motivating, and able to persevere in the face of difficulties. They tended to have successful marriages, higher incomes, greater career satisfaction, better health, and reported more fulfilling lives than "non-resisters." The "non-resisters," as adults, tended to be more troubled, stubborn, indecisive, mistrustful, and less self- confident.

Over the past fifty years as the field of emotional intelligence has grown, thousands of studies shed light on specific EQ skills, and how to learn, build, and improve them. Insights from these studies are transforming how schools teach, how parents parent, and how we all can function better and happier.

The Connection Between God And Emotional Intelligence
God is more mysterious than humans can comprehend, but we know from our own experiences that whomever and whatever God is, God is with us and within us. We have experienced God in the strength that

comes when are weak, the joy we feel when we are with loved ones, the smile of a stranger, the kindness of a friend, the laugh of a child, the solace of memories, the excitement of new plans.

Meister Eckert, a thirteenth-century German theologian, described the divinity within us as a "God Spark" which he defined as the "yearning experienced by every human being to be a part of something larger than ourselves."[3] The theme flowing through this book is that emotional intelligence is one way all human beings can nurture the God spark within each of us. Through the stories of this book, we see that emotions nurture our "God Spark" by providing us with important information. Positive emotions like joy, happiness, and contentment tell us that what we are doing, or who we are with, are good for us. Empathy tells us not to judge ourselves or others too harshly. Forgiveness teaches us to forgive others and ourselves. Negative emotions, which Sue Monk Kidd describes as "angels that disturb the waters of our soul,"[4] also guide us. Fear warns us of danger. Sadness saps our energy, keeping us still, protecting us, so we do not venture forth when we are unable to make wise decisions. Anxiety tells us to manage our stress better. In these ways, emotional intelligence is one of the "resources" God gives us for our earthy and spiritual journeys.

Let us turn to one example from the Bible that shows lessons in emotional intelligence. David, a boy shepherd, became a powerful king. As a young man, David demonstrated exceptional emotional intelligence in controlling his negative emotions. For example, he did not let fear consume him when he faced Goliath, or resentment and fury overtake him when Saul, a person he trusted, set out to kill him. David grew into a calm, wise, and inspiring leader.

However, David was not able to exercise emotional intelligence in all aspects of his life. When he saw Bathsheba on the rooftop, he let passion, arrogance, and greed overtake his judgment. He lost his moral compass when, for selfish reasons, he ordered the murder of a good person — Uriah, Bathsheba's husband. As an elderly man, David sunk into despair when another person he trusted, his beloved son, Absalom, turned on him.

David's story teaches us a fundamental lesson about emotional intelligence — that however excellent our emotional intelligence at some points, or in some aspects of our lives, we will suffer when we are unable to exercise it. The emotional intelligence lessons continue: Paul, for all of his volatility, demonstrates excellent stress management skills; the woman accused of adultery, with Jesus's help, shows us how to manage negative emotions; Joseph teaches resilience, Moses exemplifies self-awareness; Job demonstrates how to use strengths and manage weaknesses; Naomi and Ruth teach us adaptability; Noah shows how to practice gratitude; Jesus models for us virtually every emotional intelligence skill.

For Those Who Wonder About The "God Stuff"
When we started gathering information for this book, we envisioned it as appealing primarily to people of faith. We did not anticipate that it may resonate with skeptics of God, faith, or religion. But something kept happening through conversations we had while we were working on this book. These conversations came up at social or work events, even at some family events. We did not bring up this book or initiate conversations about it because these were not the type of events where one would talk about God. Nevertheless, despite our intentions to avoid "God talk," the question, "What are you up to these days?" sometimes brought up this book. Usually, we could skirt the question with a vague answer or deflect it by talking about something else. But sometimes the person with whom we were visiting pushed for more information, and when they did, we would tell them a bit about this book.

To a person, they were intrigued. It was interesting for us to see how these inquiring folks tended to fall into three groups. The first group more or less consisted of individuals who were somewhat, or very, religious and inclined to believe that God actively intervenes in human lives. To them the notion that emotions and the ability to intelligently manage emotions are gifts from God was no big deal. It was consistent with their sense that God is actively involved in our lives.

The second group generally consisted of people who may or may not go to church or may or may not spend much time or energy thinking about spiritual matters but tended to have a sense of God as a "higher power." To these individuals, the idea that the Bible contains practical wisdom on how to manage emotions also was no big deal. Such a view was consistent with their belief that there is a "higher power" bringing a centeredness and steadiness to life. To them, emotional intelligence was another tool in the toolbox, along with meditation, readings, yoga, and for some, church.

The people in both of these groups were curious and probing but did not seem surprised by the premise of our book. What we did not anticipate was the interest in this book by a third group, those to whom the idea that the Bible might have practical application to today's world was bizarre. These folks tended to ask the most questions. Many told us that viewing the Bible as providing insight into human behavior was the first time they thought of the Bible as having any applicability to them or to modern life. As one friend put it, "this EQ and the Bible stuff makes me think there might be something on the other side of the door."

The genuine interest and probing questions of our spiritually curious friends opened our eyes to see that emotional intelligence, maybe because it has permeated our modern culture, may be a route for everyone, churched or unchurched, believer or nonbeliever, to access the power of the Bible.

The Story Of This Book ... And One Thing It Has Taught Us

To be honest, it is difficult for us to share what lies ahead in this section. Doing so requires something neither of us is very comfortable with. As academics for a large part of our careers, we have both been pretty successful in cloaking our personal lives in facts, lectures, presentations, meetings, and conferences. But this book has forced a change in our modus operandi. As we asked others to share their stories for this book and as we saw how their stories have grabbed hold of us, taking our souls on spiritual journeys we did not anticipate, we knew we could not ask others to do what we would not do. And so, like little children learning to swim, we took a deep breath and jumped. We hope that our newbie attempts at being honest about our hopes, fears, joys, and vulnerabilities will encourage you to ponder more deeply your life and see on what spiritual journey that may take yo. In this section, you will hear first from Pam, then from Cathy, then from both of us. In Chapter Six (Habits) you will hear from Pam and in Chapter Thirteen (Gratitude) you will hear from Cathy.

Pam: I am a "preacher's kid," raised as a Presbyterian. I loved going to church where I had lots of friends and got to eat incredible scalloped potatoes at Wednesday night covered dish suppers. As an adult, I became a Methodist because that's where my kids' friends went and where my kids wanted to go. I loved being a Methodist, especially teaching wiggly, squirming teenagers. I discovered the beauty of Catholic mass when my son became a student at Holy Spirit Catholic School in Tuscaloosa, Alabama. Eventually, I found my way to the

Episcopal church. One thing that has remained the same throughout my faith journey is that I'm always full of questions about how all this "God stuff" works and how my faith applies in day-to-day life. Thankfully, I have been surrounded by kind, patient people who never tired of my questions.

Beginning my career as a federal prosecutor trying white collar criminal cases, I later became a law school professor. On the first day of criminal law class, every law student is eager and excited to be in law school, full of energy, and even if nervous, abundantly confident that he or she will be as successful in the years ahead as in the past.

Having taught for thirty-plus years, I see former law students everywhere I go. Sometimes twenty or more years may have passed since I last saw them. Many still have the energy, excitement, and joy they had when I first met them. But some bear no resemblance to the vibrant, hopeful, happy people they were when they entered law school. Although many have positions of prestige, their voices are weary, their faces are sad, their shoulders sag as they tell me what they are doing. They are empty shells of their former selves.

Distressed at seeing this too often, I began to wonder if I could create a program or course in law school that may help students choose careers that would bring them personal as well as professional satisfaction. I put together a new course, wrote a book to use in teaching it, and conducted several empirical studies on stress and lawyers. Economics and finance are part of this course, but so is emotional intelligence. Developing this course was, to be honest, my first real exposure to the field of behavioral science. At the time, the notion of emotional intelligence was relatively new and was utterly foreign to me. I was amazed as I learned about the wisdom and science of it and the practical, helpful information it offers.

Inevitably, as do we all, I ran into some difficult times in my life. At some point during one of these hard times, I realized that I was handling things differently than I had in the past — that I was in fact using what I had learned about emotional intelligence in my course for law students. I also kept having the feeling, *I've seen this somewhere before*, and one day it hit me. The emotional intelligence I was learning reminded me of the Bible stories with which I had grown up. And with that, the stories I had not really paid attention to came to life. I saw that the Bible was full of people just like me who experienced confusion, fear, sadness, emptiness, purpose, joy, love, and at times, inner peace.

God works in peculiar ways. What I thought I was doing to help law students was God's way of helping me learn how to stay afloat when the big waves came my way.

One night at book club as Cathy and I were stacking dinner dishes, I asked if she might be interested in writing a book together on emotional intelligence and the Bible. Thankfully, she said yes.

Cathy: After having grown up in the Presbyterian room of God's house, the Episcopal Church became my church home when I married a faithful Episcopalian. Its comfort with mystery and the beauty of its liturgy were major attractions. It has nurtured me on my spiritual journey into retirement as the director of a university's honors programs and continues to nurture our three children and four grandchildren.

When Pam suggested that we write this book, I gave thanks for the privilege of exploring the qualities of emotional intelligence in the lives of Biblical characters that have brought me the abundant life that is God's will for all of us. Studying emotional intelligence validated the critical importance of strengthening our emotional intelligence as we grow into the people God created us to be.

Decades ago, I was confronted with an amazing concept: perhaps negative emotions were God's gift to us when we left the Garden of Eden. Without fear, wild beasts would have devoured Adam and Eve quickly. Without anxiety, they might not have made long term plans. Daniel Goleman, one of the foremost behavioral scientists studying emotional intelligence, describes anxiety as "a presumed utility in evolution…but in modern life, anxiety is more often out of proportion and out of place."[5] In today's world, anxiety may not be a survival instinct but may be harmful by taking a toll on the immune system and the cardiovascular system, making us more susceptible to illness. "But if chronic emotional distress in its many forms is toxic," Goleman continues, "the opposite range of emotion can be *tonic*… hope has healing power."[6] Learning basic emotional intelligence skills so that they become lifelong habits enables and empowers us to process instinctual negative emotions more rapidly, making room in our hearts for the joy for which our creator made us. These habits can impart a sense of control, removing the anxiety caused by the lack of control of our lives that we often feel. Allowing negative emotions to continue seems almost selfish: burdened by them, we have less capacity to reach out in love to others.

I hope that by studying the emotional intelligence traits that were effective in the lives of biblical as well as contemporary heroes/heroines, we can all be inspired, encouraged, and empowered to relinquish negative emotions into the loving arms of our God and to replace them in our hearts with emotional intelligence habits that make us more of the people God created us to be.

Pam and Cathy: Throughout our professional lives, we have learned about emotional intelligence in the contexts of law, business, community relations, higher education, and philanthropy. In the peaks and valleys of our personal lives we have learned more. We have been captivated by how a new discipline, made possible with twenty-first-century tools, demonstrates, once again, the wisdom of Bible stories from thousands of years ago.

Developing emotional intelligence, we have seen, is not a speedy exercise. There is seldom a quick road to happiness in any experience in life. Yes, many psalms begin with a lament and end with praise, but while in life, the distance between the two is not as short. Emotional intelligence can help shorten it.

How This Book Is Organized

There are fourteen chapters in this book: this introduction, twelve chapters on twelve topics of emotional intelligence, and a conclusion. Each chapter has four sections: the story of a person of the Bible; an overview of the behavioral science regarding the emotional intelligence skill profiled in the chapter; the story of a modern day person; and a section, "The Ties That Bind," that links the behavioral science to the two stories, showing how both the biblical person and the modern-day person used the emotional intelligence skill of the chapter. The concluding chapter provides an all-encompassing review of the book, drawing parallels among those we profile, and tying the stories together to show emotional intelligence as the foundation for all humans' spiritual searching and connection.

Each chapter ends with questions for thought and reflection, and suggested exercises and practices. Appendix A, the ancient practice of *Lectio Divina*, a traditional monastic practice, is an opportunity to explore each chapter even deeper with meditation or prayer. Appendix B is a step-by-step guide for mindfulness meditation. This book works well for an individual reader, adult and young adult Christian education classes, book clubs, mental health professionals in need of resources for clients, and, as we now know thanks to those who open our eyes, skeptics who are curious if "there is something behind the door."

We hope that you enjoy reading this book as much as we have enjoyed writing it.

Questions For Thought And Reflection

1. What has been your experience with the Bible? A lot? None? Meaningful? Engaging? Which Bible stories stick in your mind? Why these?

2. Have you heard of emotional intelligence? Where did you hear about it? What is your sense, at this point, about what constitutes emotional intelligence? As you read further, consider whether your understanding of emotional intelligence may be changing.

3. Thankfully, for those of us who would be among the two-thirds of four-year-old's who cannot resist eating the marshmallow right away, emotional intelligence skills can be taught, learned, and strengthened throughout life, regardless of our "EQ deficiencies" early in life or, like David, our "EQ lapses" throughout our lives. Using the list of emotional intelligence skills in the Table of Contents, assess yourself as to each skill with "1" for "use this a lot," "2" for "use this some of the time," and "3" for "could use improvement." At the conclusion of this book, reassess yourself.

4. The "God Spark"
   - Have you ever yearned to feel part of something larger than yourself? When have you experienced this?
   - Have you ever felt that there is more to life than simply existing? Can you recall when you first felt this? What prompted it? Do any experiences in your life now prompt this feeling? What are they?
   - Have you ever felt a "sense of beyond" by the love you have for another or that which another has shown you?
   - Have you felt uplifted by the kindness of another person, a

beautiful sunset, a strength that came over you when you were depleted, weary and in need of strength?

- Do you believe these moments are a "God Spark," a bit of divinity within you?
- Would you like to have more of these moments?

CHAPTER TWO: MANAGING STRESS

This chapter discusses how to manage stress by looking at the traits of individuals whom behavioral scientists have identified as "stress hardy." By developing and implementing these traits, we learn how to manage stress without the lasting negative physical, psychological, or emotional costs of stress. We focus on the stories of Paul in the New Testament and of Bryan Stevenson, a lawyer, author, and advocate for criminal justice reform and those on death row.

Paul

Paul, the Apostle, began his life as Saul. He was born in the year 7 CE into a wealthy family in the city of Tarsus, a vibrant commercial city on the coast of modern-day Turkey. Saul's family owned and operated a lucrative tent-making business. Saul grew up in comfort and prestige, and with an education available only to sons of wealthy families. The Jewish community in Tarsus, estimated in Saul's day to be 7,000, was large and vibrant. Prominent Jewish families, such as Saul's, were granted Roman citizenship which conferred significant advantages such as the ability to conduct business to the Roman army.[7]

At the age of twenty-one, Saul moved to Jerusalem where he trained to become a Pharisaic rabbi. Saul became a vigorous persecutor of Jesus' followers dragging men and women to prison. On a trip to Damascus in a hunt for followers of Jesus, Saul had a vision that led him to become a follower of Jesus:

> "Saul, still breathing threats and murder against the disciples of the Lord was approaching Damascus when suddenly a light from heaven flashed around him and he heard a voice saying to him, 'Saul, Saul, why do you persecute me?' ... For three days, Saul was without sight.... The Lord came to Ananias, a disciple in Damascus and said to him in a vision,' I have chosen Saul to bring my name before Gentiles and kings and before the people of Israel.'
>
> ...Saul began to proclaim Jesus in the synagogues, saying, 'he is the Son of God'" (Excerpted from Acts 9:1-22).

Some followers of Jesus, believing Paul's conversion to be a ruse to persecute them, wanted to apprehend and kill him. Others, also Jesus' supporters but who had come to trust Paul, lowered Paul in a basket through an opening in the city wall. Fleeing to Jerusalem, Paul was again threatened with death and fled, beginning years of persecution as he traveled throughout Arabia and Syria spreading the word of Jesus.

During his ministry, Paul popularized Jesus' message through his letters and preaching, opened Christianity to Gentiles, established hundreds of church communities throughout Asia, Greece, and Rome, and focused Christian doctrine on Jesus' teachings of mercy. Paul is recognized as perhaps the greatest apostle of all time.[8]

Behavioral Science Of Stress: The Biology Of Stress

We all know that stress creates emotional turmoil. It also has a significant physical impact. Our bodies were created to survive in the stressful environments in which our ancestors lived, such as jungles, forests, and deserts. In those times, people needed to be able to run away from predators and essential to survival was a physical stress response activated by dramatic bodily changes when one senses danger. This stress response and its impact on the human body enables humans to run away, fight, or otherwise protect themselves from peril.

Although our modern-day lives have changed dramatically from our ancestors, we have the same biological stress response as did humans thousands of years ago.[9] Our body's stress response begins when our adrenal glands, located above the kidneys, shoot two hormones, adrenaline and cortisol, throughout our bodies. These hormones increase our heart rate and blood pressure, pumping oxygen-rich blood to our large muscles so we can run faster and jump higher. Our digestive system shuts down to divert more blood to our large muscles. Blood flows away from our skin to our large muscles to give us a burst of speed. Insulin production in our pancreas, liver, muscles, and fatty tissues is inhibited to give us immediate energy. Our brains release "neuropeptide S," which sharpens our senses of sight, hearing, and smell, and increases our anxiety (anxiety gives a sense of urgency to act).

Our biological response to danger, while essential to survival when we lived in jungles, forests, or deserts, and still essential in a short-term situation of stress such as a car accident, does not serve us well in modern life. [10] Think back to times of intense stress you have experienced. Maybe it was a call from the police at 2 am that your child was in custody. Maybe it was being in a car accident. Maybe it was losing your job. Recall the rush of adrenalin, the terrible feeling in the pit of your stomach, the sense that your skin was crawling, the exhaustion when things finally calmed down.

The human body's response to acute stress is dramatic and essential to our survival but it will harm us if it lasts more than a few minutes or occurs frequently.[11] A prolonged rush of adrenaline scars our blood vessels, clogs our arteries, and may contribute to heart attacks and strokes. Elevated levels of cortisol suppress our immune system, leading to autoimmune diseases such as asthma and diabetes. [12] When our digestive system shuts down to divert blood to our large muscles, we become constipated; or get diarrhea,[13] irritable bowel syndrome, or peptic ulcers. When blood flows away from our skin to our large muscles, we get skin disorders such as fever blisters, eczema, psoriasis, hives, and rosacea.[14]

The elevated levels of adrenalin and cortisol that kick-start our body's stress response are also bad for our brains. To supply our bodies with adrenalin and cortisol, our brain diverts blood from the hippocampus, which governs memory and cognitive function to other parts of our brain that govern our senses of sight, sound and smell [occipital lobe (vision), temporal lobe (sound), and olfactory lobe (smell)].[15] However, diverting blood from our hippocampus results in foggy thinking (individuals with high level of stress perform 50% worse on cognitive tests than when they are not under stress). Over time chronic stress causes the hippocampus to shrink which correlates with dementia and Alzheimer's disease. [16]

The elevated levels of adrenalin and cortisol that occur when our bodies respond to stress also make us depressed. Dopamine and magnesium, which we need to regulate hormones essential to our emotional wellbeing, are needed to generate the adrenalin and cortisol demanded by our bodies' stress response. Chronic stress depletes these hormones which in turn causes depression.[17] For these reasons, the human body, which is amazingly effective in handling immediate, short-term stress is not well suited to modern lives of chronic worry, rushing around, and sleep deprivation.

How To Become Stress Hardy
Not surprisingly, behavioral scientists have studied the human stress

response and effective ways to manage stress. They have done so by studying different groups under considerable stress such as deployed US Military personnel, West Point Military Academy cadets, recent immigrants, undergraduate college students, self-employed management consultants, high school basketball players, and nurses in hospital operating theatres and hospice. All of these studies consistently show that some percentage of people in stressful situations are "stress hardy." These individuals do not experience the physical, psychological, or emotional costs of stress as do the rest of us.

In studying these stress hardy individuals, behavioral scientists have learned that there are no demographic traits that correlate to stress hardiness: not wealth, health, physical attractiveness, gender, race, or geography. What the studies have shown is that stress hardy individuals possess three behavioral traits that help them manage stress: a sense of control, a sense of purpose, and cognitive flexibility.[18]

Sense of control: Maintaining a sense of control is not the same as having control of a situation. At some point, none of us can control the events in our lives, but each of us can seek to control how we respond to these events. As Victor Frankel said, "Everything can be taken from a man but one thing: the last of the human freedoms—to choose one's attitude in any given set of circumstances, to choose one's own way." [19] Recognizing what we have control over and what we do not minimizes stress by calming us and directing our attention to what we can do in any situation, however dire the situation may be.

Sense of purpose: The second trait of stress hardy individuals is a sense of purpose, which as noted throughout this book, is consistently found to be "the most reliable predictor of psychological well-being at every stage of the life span, from adolescence to late adulthood."[20] Knowing that we are needed, valued, and contributing to make the world a better place even if it is something as small as a kind word to someone who is having a hard time, makes us all feel better. A sense of purpose minimizes stress by giving us perspective about what is important and what is not. The home repairs that may have consumed us cease to be important if our child is seriously injured in a car accident. The project we have been obsessing over at work means very little when a hurricane is coming.

Cognitive Flexibility: Cognitive flexibility, also and not surprisingly important in other emotional intelligence skills (particularly, resilience and adaptability), is the third trait of stress-hardy individuals. In the context of managing stress, such flexibility is recognizing when circumstances have changed and what adjustments need to be made to adapt. This ability to pivot and seek a new direction or revise goals minimizes stress by helping us see constructive steps we can take, which in turn, gives us a sense of control.

Bryan

Bryan Stevenson was born in 1958 in a poor area of rural Delaware where schools and businesses were segregated, and confederate flags flew. Bryan's father worked in a factory and cleaned beach rentals on weekends. His mother worked as an Air Force civilian. Bryan did well academically, earned scholarships, attended a small college in Pennsylvania, and went to Harvard Law School. By the end of his first year of law school, Bryan was disillusioned with what he saw as his career trajectory (corporate law) and questioning whether a career in law was for him. After a one-month internship at a public interest law office in Atlanta, Bryan found a type of legal practice that was meaningful and purposeful for him. [21] His internship, at the Southern Prisoners Defense Committee (SPDC), was devoted to representing individuals who had been sentenced to the death penalty. In 1985, Bryan, upon his law school graduation, moved to Atlanta and began working at SPDC.

Shortly after moving, Bryan learned what it was like to be a Black man living in the deep south. One evening, about midnight, arriving home late after a long day of traveling, Bryan parked outside his home. As he sat in his car gathering his legal files, his car was suddenly surrounded by Atlanta SWAT officers. They drew their weapons as one officer shouted, "Move, and I'll blow your head off!" Trying to calm the officer, Bryan repeated over and over, "It's all right. It's okay; it's okay. I live here." The officer, a white man about Bryan's height, continued to point his gun at Bryan's head while a second officer grabbed Bryan by the arms and pushed him against the back of his car.[22]

The officers searched Bryan and his car, scattering his work files throughout his car and onto the sidewalk. Neighbors came out of their homes and watched, talking among themselves about burglaries in the neighborhood. Bryan recalls hearing an older white woman loudly demand that he be questioned about items she was missing. "Ask him about my radio and vacuum cleaner!" she yelled. Eventually the officers satisfied themselves that Bryan was who he claimed and left.

Three years after joining SPDC, Bryan moved to Alabama to establish the Equal Justice Initiative (EJI), a public interest law firm devoted to representing defendants on death row. Shortly after opening EJI, the support and funding promised for its operation disappeared. Bryan scrambled to find other funding and relocated EJI to another city in Alabama (Montgomery). Although EJI's financial resources had dried up, EJI's docket kept expanding as the rate of executions in Alabama rose. EJI's situation became dire. The office was understaffed and cold in the winter; it didn't have enough electricity to run the copier and a coffeepot at the same time without blowing a fuse.[23]

Some people in Montgomery were hostile and racist toward EJI and its staff. One judge told Bryan, "I'm pretty fed up with people always talking about minority rights. When is someone going to come to my courtroom and protect the rights of Confederate Americans?" Bryan's life was threatened multiple times. One phone caller hissed, "You're going to be a dead nigger." In another, the caller growled, "I want y'all to stop doing what you're doing. My first option is not to kill everybody, so you better get out of there now! Next time there won't be a warning."[24] EJI staff repeatedly had to evacuate their offices because of bomb threats.

Doing his job was a challenge. Once Bryan was stopped by a deputy sheriff as he tried to enter the courtroom where he was the attorney of record. Unlike the white attorneys who were patted down when they went into Alabama prisons to see their clients, Bryan was told by a prison official, "You're going to go into that bathroom and take everything off if you expect to get into my prison." Bryan tried to explain, "I think you might be confused. I'm an attorney. Lawyers don't have to get strip-searched to come in for legal visits." The correctional officer refused to budge. Bryan was forced to comply.

Despite the hostility in the community and from many in the judicial system, EJI grew, as did the roles Bryan undertook. In 2014 Bryan's book, *Just Mercy*, was published, becoming a *New York Times* bestseller and receiving multiple book awards. In 2019, it was made into a major motion picture with outstanding reviews from audiences worldwide. It was heralded as "a powerful, bold true story about the potential for mercy to redeem us and a clarion call to fix American's broken system of justice from one of the most brilliant and influential lawyers of our time." [25] Seeing that there was no institution in the United States that told the history of the slave trade and the legacy of slavery in the U.S.,

Bryan and EJI founded *The Legacy Museum: From Enslavement to Mass Incarceration* in Montgomery, Alabama. The museum documents slavery's history in the United States and provides educational programs, attracting 400,000 visitors each year.[26]

The Ties That Bind: Stress Management Skills In Day-To-Day Life

Let us look at some of the ways both Paul and Bryan managed stress for they both had plenty of it. Paul suffered multiple beatings, a shipwreck, multiple imprisonments, distrust among Jesus's followers even after his conversion, and even rejection by some of the churches he had established and friends he had made. Bryan experienced physical threats, setbacks, racism, discrimination, and constant challenges in his law practice and in expanding EJI to include worldwide community outreach. He maintains a physically and emotionally grueling practice of law, yet makes time to write, and expand EJI's mission to raise awareness of racial injustice.

How do we see Paul and Bryan demonstrating stress-hardiness? Paul could not control the murderous crowds that sought to kill him or the hardships and disappointments that came his way, but he could control how he responded to these events by focusing on actions he could control. He relied on prayer, his faith, and his skills. He preached, he taught, he founded churches. When he was imprisoned, he wrote of Jesus's teachings, impacting forever the growth of Christianity. Similarly, Bryan could not control the injustices he saw, and sees, but he uses his skills to bring racial justice to the world by representing those condemned to die. He tells their story not just in court, but by writing, speaking, and traveling worldwide.

Paul and Bryan both had (and have) a sense of purpose. When Paul encountered obstacles his sense of purpose held him up. He found solace in spreading the news of the loving God of grace about whom Jesus taught. As Paul wrote to his friends in Philippi: "Do not be anxious about anything, but in everything by prayer and supplication with thanksgiving let your requests be made known to God."

Similarly, Bryan finds a sense of purpose that gives him strength.[27] In *Just Mercy*, Bryan describes an occasion when he was at his office late, on the phone with Jimmy Dill, a client who was on death row. Jimmy was scheduled to die in a few hours. As Bryan recounts: "Listening to him was hard. Jimmy's stuttering was worse than usual, and he was having great difficulty getting his words out. He was scared, but he was trying valiantly to express his gratitude for our efforts. It was heartbreaking. I was crying."[28] Bryan asked himself, "Why am I doing this? I can just leave." At that moment, Paul's words came to him: "Three times I appealed to the Lord about this, that it would leave me, but he said to me, 'My grace is sufficient for you, for power is made perfect in weakness.' "[29] Bryan describes the feeling that came over him:

> *"I do what I do because I'm broken....We are all broken by something. We have all hurt someone and have been hurt. Our shared brokenness connects us. I am more than broken. In fact, there is a strength, a power even, in understanding brokenness, because embracing our brokenness creates a need and desire for mercy, and perhaps a corresponding need to show mercy. When you experience mercy, you see things you can't otherwise see. You hear things you can't otherwise hear. You begin to recognize the humanity that resides in each of us. The power of mercy is that it belongs to the undeserving. It has the power to heal."*[30]

Bryan left his office that night and drove home, "broken and brokenhearted about Jimmy Dill, but knowing that I would come back the next day because there was more work to do."

Note how both Paul and Bryan demonstrated cognitive flexibility in managing stress. They were able to pivot when obstacles appeared; they saw new directions, new avenues for action, new ways of approaching their goals. When Jesus came to Paul in a vision, Paul changed the course of his life. No longer a persecutor of Jesus's followers, Paul became the greatest apostle of Jesus. When hostile crowds ran him out of town after town, Paul moved on and spread the gospel to new communities and new nations, to Gentiles as well as to Jews. When imprisoned and unable to personally carry Jesus's message, Paul changed his way of reaching audiences. He wrote, and thankfully he did. Paul's letters, his "back up" to traveling personally, became an even greater ministry, lasting thousands of years.

Bryan has similarly displayed remarkable flexibility when confronting obstacles. When promised funding for EJI failed to materialize, Bryan found other funding and moved EJI's offices to another city. When government funding was cancelled, he raised private funds. When his clients are convicted unfairly, Bryan appealed their cases to more courts, making new arguments. When he saw that there was no historical chronicle of the racial terror of lynchings in the United States, Bryan and EJI expanded the mission of EJI beyond legal representation of clients to establish a world-famous museum documenting the human cost of legalized racial segregation and racial hierarchy in America.

As an aside, an additional lesson in Paul's story teaches us something about lessons about emotional intelligence in general. Paul did not always display emotional intelligence, whether regarding stress management skills, empathy, or compassion. He, like us, had to grow in his emotional intelligence. At times, Paul lashed out to those to whom he ministered. For example, furious at the churches of Galatia (which he had founded) for turning to apostles other than himself who, according to Paul, "wanted to pervert the gospel of Christ" (Galatians 1:7), Paul rails and rants: "You foolish Galatians! I am astonished that you are so quickly deserting the one who called you in the grace of Christ" (Gal 3:1, 1:6). On another occasion, after recounting the sacrifices he had made to bring Christ's message to the Galatians and feeling woefully underappreciated, Paul wallows in self-pity, "I am afraid my work for you may have been wasted" (Galatians 4:11). At times, he was unable to contain his anger, sounding like a child having a tantrum: "From now on, let no one make trouble for me." (Galatians 6:17), wishing that those who were "perverting the gospel of Christ" …. "would castrate themselves." (Galatians 5:15).

The Bible's honest portrayal of Paul, the good and the flawed, allows us to see another human who, just like us, says and does things in haste, in anger. It allows us to see a beautiful example of God's grace — for Paul, and for ourselves. God never gave up on Paul, despite his shortcomings. The same is true for us. God never gives up on us.

Conclusion
Paul and Bryan serve as wonderful role models for how to manage stress. Their lives show us how to focus on what we can control rather than become overwhelmed by what we cannot control; how to find and anchor ourselves in purpose; and how to pivot and make changes in the face of obstacles that arise. By following Paul's and Bryan's examples, we too can become stress-hardy.

We close this chapter with the words of Henry, a prisoner on death row whom Bryan met when he was a law student. After Bryan and Henry had visited for several hours in a Georgia prison, a prison guard came to lead Henry away. Henry's response tells us what we need to know about emotional intelligence. Bryan describes what happened: "The guard was shoving him roughly toward the door. Henry continued to smile until just before the guard could push him fully out of the room, he planted his feet to resist the officer's shoving, closed his eyes, tilted his head back, and began to sing:

> "I'm pressing on, the upward way,
> New heights I'm gaining, every day,
> Still praying as, I'm onward bound,
> Lord, plant my feet on higher ground" [31]

Questions For Thought And Reflection

1. Think about the night Bryan was in his office on the phone with Jimmy Dill, and how Paul's words came to Bryan, right when he felt overwhelmed and tempted to leave his career. Paul's words gave Bryan strength to persevere. Have you experienced times when you felt beaten, worn down, unable to carry on, and something beyond you — words from a family member, a friend, a teacher, a book, a song, a feeling, a memory — came over you and gave you strength? Was this God reaching out to you?

2. Paul and Bryan found strength to handle the demands they faced by extending God's mercy to others. What does it mean "to extend God's mercy to others"? Have you received mercy? From whom? Have you extended mercy to another? How do we extend mercy to ourselves?

3. Not sure if you're stressed? Here are some clues:
   - Tight neck or jaw muscles
   - Tight shoulders or back
   - Jutted-out chin
   - Gritting or grinding of teeth
   - Tight, strained voice
   - Hunched shoulders
   - Tightly curled toes or fingers
   - Drumming with your fingers

- Foot tapping, legs constantly in motion
- Rigid spine
- Tight forehead muscles, sometimes with a headache
- Sweating hands, feet, or armpits
- Irritability, overreacting to small things
- Frowning
- High pulse rate, heart pounding rapidly
- Brusque, jerky movements with muscles tight or braced
- Irregular, shallow breathing or sighing respiration
- Feeling of suffocation
- Nervous stomach, cramping, or nausea
- Urinating frequently
- Smoking intensely
- Fluttering eyes or eyestrain.[32]

4. How do we bring unnecessary stress upon ourselves?

5. Stress hardiness can be learned, practiced, and strengthened. Are there ways you can strengthen your sense of control when in a situation beyond your control? Your sense of purpose? Your ability to be creative and flexible when encountering impasses in life?

6. Note what Paul's and Bryan's lives teach us about having purpose in life.
    - Some days it will be really hard to sense a purpose in life. Our lives may seem ordinary. We may not face shipwrecks or imprisonment, racism, hostility, but we all face obstacles, quandaries, disappointments that bring us to our knees. What in Paul's life and Bryan's life resonates with you about finding and staying anchored to a sense of purpose?
    - Rarely is "our purpose in life" self-evident. Paul was struck blind before he found his purpose in life. Bryan had to experience disappointment in his career before he found his purpose. How have you found purpose after encountering disappointment? How so?

- As much as the lives of Paul and Bryan teach us about purpose in life, there is one thing they do not model for us. It is safe to say that few or none of us will be acknowledged as the "greatest apostle of all time" or become today's Atticus Finch, a bestselling author, visionary, and modern-day prophet. Thankfully, a worthy purpose in life does not require such heroic feats. Being kind to another person is a worthy purpose. Showing up day in and day out is worthy. Caring for family and friends is worthy. Stopping to savor the wonder and glory of being alive is worthy. These mundane acts add up. What are the "little" opportunities for seeing purpose in your life?

CHAPTER THREE: DEALING WITH NEGATIVE EMOTIONS

This chapter focuses on the elephant in the room, actually, for most of us, the elephant on our laps. We all experience negative emotions — anger, fear, envy, anxiety, self-pity, shame. The list is endless. Yet if we cannot manage the negative emotions that can hijack us, we can't use our emotional intelligence skills however well-honed they may be. This chapter looks at the science of managing negative emotions. Using the New Testament story of the woman accused of adultery and the journey of Nick and his family when Nick was arrested on felony drug charges, we focus on one negative emotion, shame, to demonstrate how three strategies of emotional intelligence can help us overcome and grow from any negative emotion.

The Woman Accused Of Adultery
The public shame at being found out and brought before a crowd of angry people full of judgment must be truly awful. This was the fate of the woman accused of adultery:

> *"Jesus returned to the Mount of Olives, but early the next morning he was back again at the temple. A crowd soon gathered, and he sat down and taught them. As he was speaking, the teachers of religious law and the Pharisees brought a woman who had been caught in the act of adultery. They put her in front of the crowd. "'Teacher,' they said to Jesus, 'this woman was caught in the act of adultery. The law of Moses says to stone her. What do you say?' They were trying to trap him into saying something they could use against him, but Jesus stooped down and wrote in the dust with his finger.*
>
> *"They kept demanding an answer, so he stood up again and said, 'All right, but let the one who has never sinned throw the first stone!' Then he stooped down again and wrote in the dust. "When the accusers heard this, they slipped away one by one, beginning with the oldest, until only Jesus was left in the middle of the crowd with the woman. Then Jesus stood up again and said to the woman, 'Where are your accusers? Didn't even one of them condemn you?' 'No, Lord,' she said. And Jesus said, 'Neither do I. Go and sin no more.'" John 8:1-11*

Was the woman an adulterer? Perhaps. Was stoning an accepted practice in first-century Palestine for adultery? Apparently so, according to rabbinic laws of that time. But imagine the woman's embarrassment, humiliation, and fear. Note how Jesus's words sent away the crowd and he freed the woman from shame. Jesus asked the woman "Where are your accusers? Didn't even one of them condemn you?" When she said, "No, Lord," he answered her, "Neither do I. Go and sin no more." In these few words, Jesus told the woman, in essence, "Go forward. Do not walk in shame. What you have done is behind you. Hold your head up." And Jesus gave the woman important and practical advice: "Sin no more."

Let's look at the emotional intelligence Jesus taught in this encounter. Jesus offered healing to the woman in two ways. First, Jesus's lack of condemnation is unworldly. The woman, and we, expect condemnation for our faults and mistakes. We condemn ourselves regardless of whether we, like the woman, are condemned publicly. Jesus's concern was directed at the woman's self-condemnation, at the shame she felt within. He offered her freedom from her self-imposed shame.

We too, are given this gift by God. God did not come to condemn us but to love us. Consider John 3:21: "Beloved, if our hearts do not condemn us, we have confidence before God"; Psalm 37:23-24: "The Lord makes firm the steps of one who delights in him. Though he may stumble, he will not fall, for the Lord upholds him with his hand"; John 7:51: "Do not judge, and you will not be judged; do not condemn, and you will not be condemned."

The second way Jesus offered the woman healing was in admonishing her to "Go and sin no more." If the woman followed Jesus's command, what a powerful reshaping of life she must have experienced or perhaps we could even say, a remaking of her life. She was given a clean slate, a do-over that came as Jesus offered her release from shame. Jesus commanded her to leave behind her sins as well as her shame, to surrender and bury her sins in the past, and to go forward uncondemned by anyone.

Behavioral Science Of Managing Negative Emotions

Negative emotions such as shame, fear, sadness, and anger are important to survival. Shame informs us of changes we need to make in our own behavior. Fear warns us of danger. Sadness keeps us quiet and still so we can grieve and heal from traumas. Anger protects us against those who could hurt us.

However, holding onto negative emotions after they have served their purpose is not good for us: "People who experienced chronic anxiety, long periods of sadness and pessimism, unremitting tension or incessant hostility, relentless cynicism or suspiciousness, are found to have double the risk of disease."[33] But as we all know, letting go of negative emotions is easier said than done. Negative emotions are rewarding, even if in unhealthy ways. They keep us "center stage" in our internal dramas. As Frederick Buechner says of anger:

> "Of the seven deadly sins, anger is possibly the most fun. To lick your wounds, to smack your lips over grievances long past, to roll your tongue over the prospect of bitter confrontations to come, to savor to the last toothsome morsel of both the pain you are given and the pain you are giving back in many ways is a feast fit for a king."[34]

Behavioral scientists have identified strategies for dealing with negative emotions when it is time to let them go. At the heart of all these strategies is replacing negative emotions with positive emotions. Martin Seligman, the pioneer of positive psychology, explains how it is possible to "undo" negative emotions with positive emotions:

> "When people feel positive emotions, they are jolted into a different way of thinking and acting. Their thinking becomes creative and broad-minded, and their actions become adventurous and exploratory. This expanded repertoire creates more mastery over challenges, which in turn generates more positive emotion."[35]

Numerous studies show that positive emotions have a practical benefit beyond making us feel happier. Those who maintain positive emotions are more productive at work, have higher incomes, and a richer and more fulfilling social life than those with less positivity. Positive emotions help us solve life's problems: they "broaden our intellectual, physical, and social resources, building up resources we can draw upon when a threat or opportunity presents itself."[36]

An intriguing study of young children and physicians shows how positive emotions boost our problem-solving ability. A control group of four-year-olds was directed to "spend thirty seconds remembering something that happened that made you feel so happy you wanted to jump up and down." The children were then given a learning task about different shapes. The control group did better than the children who were not directed to think of a positive memory before the task. As part of the same study, a group of physicians was given candy (candy for the adults but not the kids?) before being presented with a complex case of liver disease and asked to diagnosis the problem. The "candy" group of physicians, who got a positive feeling from receiving an unexpected gift, did better in making the correct diagnosis than did the physicians who did not get candy.[37]

Positive emotions help us build social connections that are essential to our wellbeing. When we are around others, we gain practical advantages: we learn things we did not know, are exposed to information that can help us, and by meeting people gain opportunities to meet their contacts, which expands our network. And the more positive we are, the more people want to be around us: "When we are in a positive mood, people like us better and friendship, love, and coalitions are more likely to cement." [38] They sense that "our mental state is expansive, tolerant, and creative."[39]

By studying individuals who are effective at managing negative emotions behavioral scientists have identified effective strategies used by these individuals for replacing negative emotions with positive emotions. These can be identified as: (1) See the lessons embedded in bad experiences, (2) Reframe bad situations, (3) Have a sense of purpose (which not only helps manage stress, as discussed in the prior chapter) but helps manage all negative emotions.

- *Lessons Embedded in Sorrow*: No matter how dire a situation may be, we can always ask ourselves: "What is there among these broken pieces that I can use in building for the future?" Recognizing what we have going for us amid all that is going against us helps shift our negative perspective. It gives us hope. As Seligman says, "Hope is more than the sunny view that everything will turn out all right; it is believing you have both the will and the way to accomplish your goals, whatever they may be." Hope provides motivation, confidence, creative energy to break down a formidable task into smaller manageable pieces.[40] Recognizing that there is always something going for us no matter how bad things get, even if it is simply we are still alive, can give us hope.

- *Reframe*: One of the ways we can move forward from negative emotions is by "reframing" our bad situation. Reframing is one of therapy's most important skills. As one group of researchers explains:

"Negative self-talk is often an automatic reaction to stressful events. Reframing is a coping technique that assists one in becoming aware of one's internal monologue: reframing widens one's perspective of particularly challenging situations. Steps involved in reframing include becoming aware of one's thoughts, evaluating content, and challenging negative perceptions by questioning their validity."[41]

A common reframing technique is "Yes, but…" (Yes, my girlfriend broke up with me, but things weren't working so great anyway, and I can meet other people.). Note how this technique acknowledges the negative but moves beyond it. Reframing means we examine every bad situation by asking objectively, without condemnation: What mistakes did I make? What could I have done differently? What changes can I make going forward so that that doesn't happen again? This approach reframes the negative into positive in three ways. First, it "normalizes" our situation by approaching it objectively. Second, it gives us a sense of autonomy over ourselves; we need not be captives of our negative emotions. Third, it allows us to actually learn something useful.

- *Sense of Purpose*: People who lack meaning or purpose tend to suffer not only in their inability to manage stress, as we saw in the last chapter, but in their ability to handle any negative emotion. Individuals who feel little purpose in life are more likely to suffer from depression, boredom, loneliness, anxiety, and are more likely to abuse drugs. [42] Studies on sense of purpose in life are far-ranging and consistent, showing, for example, that those who break the law but report having purpose in life are less likely to re-offend than those who report low purpose in life; older adults who report having purpose in life are less likely to get Alzheimer's Disease; urban black adolescents exposed to violence who report a sense of purpose are less likely to engage in violence than those who do not report having a sense of purpose; adolescents who report a sense of purpose do better in school.[43]

  Numerous studies document ways people find a sense of purpose. These include identifying and engaging in activities in which they enjoy; setting a goal (even if small) and working towards it; doing something to help another person; interacting with or seeking advice from others who seem to have a sense of purpose; engaging in jobs or tasks that call upon our strengths. One of the most consistent ways people report finding a sense of purpose is by participating in religious study or community: "All major religious traditions provide direction regarding purpose in life, providing a perspective on what purpose is, and how it can be obtained."[44]

Kathy, Nick's Mom, Shares Her Story

"On April 13, 2000, I met my son." Kathy says. "He is beautiful, he is a miracle, even in his sweet tears he is shouting, *"Mama, I'm alive. Please love me and hold me."* His curly black hair, his deep brown eyes, and his already formed personality capture me. He is twenty years old. On this day, he returned home, broken, sick, ashamed, and in need of mercy and love." Kathy, her husband, Ray, and their son, Nick, met with an attorney upon Nick's arrest on charges of possession and trafficking of a controlled substance. The circumstances were dire, the attorney explained. There could be multiple charges filed.

Nick asked, "Okay, so tell me straight, what is the worst-case scenario?" The attorney responded, "I can't say, there is no certain way this could go." Nick persisted, "Just in your experience… what's the worst case for me?" The attorney paused. There was dead stillness. "Well, in my experience, you could get anywhere from three years to life in prison." The attorney advised that they keep everything confidential, including from Nick's younger sister, Sarah, who was in high school. "For her protection," he advised. The attorney warned of potential retaliation against Nick and his family by those with whom Nick bought and sold drugs. The attorney — and the police — gave Nick instructions: "Stay at your parents' house; do not leave; keep your phone by your side."

"What has happened? Is this a bad dream?" Kathy's mind screamed. "We woke up one morning and by 10:00 am realized we were dealing with police charges, the possibility of jail, drug use, and a seriously ill college child." Kathy and Ray saw in that moment that Nick's behavior, which they had naively thought was simply immature decisions, getting in the wrong crowd, not studying enough, was much more serious. Nick was an addict.

From the point of his arrest, the easy-going life Nick knew at twenty years old was over. This new world was not a game. There were police questionings and meetings with the attorney. Nick began to mention his need for medical attention. He told his parents he badly wanted to see his doctor as soon as possible. *"Your doctor?"* Kathy asked. *"I didn't know you had your own doctor!"* At Nick's insistence, Kathy placed a call to "Nick's doctor" in hopes of scheduling an appointment soon. She hoped for a callback by the end of day. Within the hour, a nurse called and said the doctor would see them at their convenience. What? Kathy thought, at our convenience?

Kathy, Ray, and Nick met with Nick's doctor. The doctor walked into the room and said, "I'm glad you're here, Mr. and Mrs. Hayes. I wanted to call you but under HIPPA regulations, I was not legally able to inform you of Nick's problem." The doctor turned to Nick, "I'm glad to see you, Nick. When you left my office the last time, I was convinced that you'd either end up in prison or dead." Kathy's mind was swirling, *"Did he just say, 'prison or dead?'"*

The doctor instructed Nick to tell his parents the truth. Nick admitted that he had been using drugs, what kind, and the amount. The doctor asked Nick if he was ready to change and pushed Nick about his level of commitment. Nick became angry. "It was painful to sit, listen, and watch the exchange," Kathy says. "I wanted the doctor to stop badgering my son; I wanted to believe Nick was telling the truth; I wanted a quick fix to make him better. I wanted this situation resolved."

The doctor calmly told them that in his opinion, Nick was a drug addict and needed to be admitted into a drug rehabilitation center immediately. "An addict?" Kathy asked. "He's only has six weeks left in this semester; he can't be pulled out of his classes." The doctor's response was calm but firm. "He cannot wait six weeks. Find a program now. Make some phone calls. Find a place. Be thankful your son is alive and will only lose six weeks of school, not his life." With that, the doctor walked out of the room. Kathy describes that "a scary reality settled in the room and moved into our minds and hearts. Our son was a drug addict. Nick was ashamed. And I was ashamed," Kathy says. "After Nick's news, I would find myself in social situations and not know how, or whether, to talk about our family crises. In my church, I told only one friend of our pain. At work, Ray did not express his great pain and concern. We were mortified that we had allowed our son to get in this situation. The shame of our failings was a burden very hard to bear. We were embarrassed and feared what people might think; we feared rejection and judgment. Shame does that to you. Shame tells you that you are unworthy, unwanted, cast away."

Over the next several years, Nick and his family worked on a difficult program of recovery and restoration. Today, years later, Nick is well, sober, has a PhD in addiction and recovery, and works to help others. His parents have been recognized nationally for their leadership in bringing campus recovery centers to colleges nationwide.[45]

At the time of Nick's arrest, the Hayes' were renowned collegiate educators. Ray served as chancellor of The University of Alabama System, one of the largest university systems in the United States. Kathy taught college freshmen. It was not easy being in such public positions and talking of their family's ordeal but instead of hiding it in a cloak of shame, Ray and Kathy chose to share it. In doing so, they helped change how the American higher education system handles addiction on campuses nationwide. Until the past ten years or so, most college campuses throughout the United States, fearful of stigma and dropping enrollments, sought to keep substance abuse by students hidden. Students were expelled, records sealed, situations ignored as young people who could have been helped, weren't. Parents who had trusted colleges with their children came to campus not for parents' weekend, but to gather the belongings of their children who died of an overdose.

By sharing their family's experience publicly to thousands of parents, families, addicts, and alcoholics, the Hayes's have brought hope, information, resources and always, endless offers to help. They have done so by telling of their family's experience rather than hiding it.

We asked Kathy why she and her family decided to tell their story when it would have been much easier not to. Here's what she said: "The learning curve in any type of dramatic, unexpected life event is steep and fast. This is true of our story. In fact, we are still on this journey. Addiction is called a family disease because every member of the family is impacted. Every relationship within the family breaks and needs healing and restoration. Every relationship experiences shame. It sounds so bleak. But there is the good news: healing is the beautiful gift within shame. Once we opened our shame to the light we shed our shackles. We grew, changed, evolved. We still are."

The Ties That Bind: Dealing With Negative Emotions In Day-To-Day Life

"Emotional lessons...can be reshaped," according to Daniel Goleman.[46] We don't know much about the woman being stoned but we know that when Jesus came upon her she was being shamed by a crowd of people in the place where she lived. To this woman, to all who witnessed their encounter, and to us, Jesus models excellent emotional intelligence. Jesus humbled the woman's accusers by telling them, "Let the one who has never sinned throw the first stone." By telling the woman that she was no longer condemned and "Go and sin no more," Jesus essentially told her, "Go. Put this behind you. Forgive yourself. Learn from this and make changes. Move forward." In this story, Jesus teaches us how to find healing in any situation no matter how bad it may be, how badly we may have behaved, or how we may be judged by others.

We saw how Nick and his family found healing in their despair. Rather than succumbing to the toxicity of shame, they chose to find the beautiful gift hidden beneath the shame. They reframed the brokenness of their lives with purpose: helping transform higher education's approach to substance abuse on campuses. They have taken what they learned and are bringing a gift of healing to hundreds of others, one person at a time.

Questions For Thought And Reflection

1. What negative emotions do you deal with?

2. What does the story of the woman caught in adultery teach you? Who are you in the crowd?

3. With whom did you identify most in the story of Nick and his family? Why?

4. Although the Psalms were written thousands of years ago, they fully capture feelings we all experience. As you consider the following Psalms which address common negative emotions, ponder these questions: Has human nature changed since the Psalms were written? If so, how so? If not, what does that tell us?

    - Self-pity ("All who hate me whisper together about me, they imagine the worst for me." Psalm 41).

    - Shame ("...the waters have come up to my neck...I am weary with my crying; my throat is parched...shame has covered my face...I am the subject of gossip for those who sit in the gate." Psalm 69)

    - Fear ("...my bones are shaking with terror...my soul is struck with terror. I am weary with my moaning...I flood my bed with tears, my couch with weeping." Psalm 6).

- Weariness ("My wounds grow foul and fester because of my foolishness. I groan because of the tumult of my heart...I am utterly spent and crushed; I groan because of the tumult of my heart." Psalm 38).

5. How are our emotions gifts from God? How is emotional intelligence a gift from God?

6. As this chapter has discussed, behavioral scientists have found three strategies to be effective in replacing negative emotions with positive emotions: 1) finding healing in our negative experiences, 2) reframing, and 3) maintaining a sense of purpose. Consider the passage below from Mark Twain's *The Adventures of Tom Sawyer*. Did Tom nail all three? How so? Do you see opportunities in your life to do likewise?

> "Hello, old chap, you got to work, hey?"
> Tom wheeled suddenly and said: "Why, it's you, Ben! I wasn't noticing."
> "Say — I'm going in a-swimming, I am. Don't you wish you could? But of course you'd druther work — wouldn't you? Course you would!"
> Tom contemplated the boy a bit, and said: "What do you call work?"
> "Why, ain't that work?"
> Tom resumed his whitewashing, and answered carelessly: "Well, maybe it is, and maybe it ain't. All I know is, it suits Tom Sawyer."
> "Oh come, now, you don't mean to let on that you like it?"
> The brush continued to move. "Like it? Well, I don't see why I oughtn't to like it. Does a boy get a chance to whitewash a fence every day?"
> That put the thing in a new light. Ben stopped nibbling his apple. Tom swept his brush daintily back and forth — stepped back to note the effect — added a touch here and there — criticized the effect again — Ben watching every move and getting more and more interested, more and more absorbed.
> Presently he said: "Say, Tom, let me whitewash a little."
> Tom considered, was about to consent; but he altered his mind:
> "No — no — I reckon it wouldn't hardly do, Ben. You see, Aunt Polly's awful particular about this fence — right here on the street, you know — but if it was the back fence I wouldn't mind and she wouldn't. Yes, she's awful particular about this fence; it's got to be done very careful; I reckon there ain't one boy in a thousand, maybe two thousand, that can do it the way it's got to be done."

"No — is that so? Oh come, now — lemme just try. Only just a little — I'd let you, if you was me, Tom."

"Ben, I'd like to, honest injun; but Aunt Polly — well, Jim wanted to do it, but she wouldn't let him; Sid wanted to do it, and she wouldn't let Sid. Now don't you see how I'm fixed?

If you was to tackle this fence and anything was to happen to it — "

"Oh, shucks, I'll be just as careful. Now lemme try. Say — I'll give you the core of my apple."

"Well, here — No, Ben, now don't. I'm afeard — " "I'll give you all of it!"

Tom gave up the brush with reluctance in his face but alacrity in his heart. And while the late steamer Big Missouri worked and sweated in the sun, the retired artist sat on a barrel in the shade close by, dangled his legs, munched his apple, and planned the slaughter of more innocents. There was no lack of material; boys happened along every little while; they came to jeer but remained to whitewash. By the time Ben was fagged out, Tom had traded the next chance to Billy Fisher for a kite, in good repair; and when he played out, Johnny Miller bought in for a dead rat and a string to swing it with — and so on, and so on, hour after hour.

And when the middle of the afternoon came, from being a poor poverty-stricken boy in the morning, Tom was literally rolling in wealth. He had besides the things before mentioned, twelve marbles, part of a jews-harp, a piece of blue bottle-glass to look through, a spool cannon, a key that wouldn't unlock anything, a fragment of chalk, a glass stopper of a decanter, a tin soldier, a couple of tadpoles, six fire-crackers, a kitten with only one eye, a brass doorknob, a dog-collar — but no dog — the handle of a knife, four pieces of orange-peel, and a dilapidated old window sash.

He had had a nice, good, idle time all the while — plenty of company — and the fence had three coats of whitewash on it! If he hadn't run out of whitewash, he would have bankrupted every boy in the village.[47]

CHAPTER FOUR: RESILIENCE

This chapter focuses on the emotional intelligence of resilience, which is the ability to bounce back from hardships, disappointments, and setbacks. It looks at the story of Joseph in the Old Testament, the behavioral science of resilience, and the life of Liz Huntley, a mother, wife, lawyer, and nationally renowned education advocate. Behavioral scientists who have studied resilience have identified ten strategies that resilient individuals display; this chapter focuses on three of these strategies.

Joseph

Joseph was born around 1600-1700 BC in Canaan, which is modern day Palestine, Syria, and Israel. Joseph's parents were Jacob and Rachel. Jacob had many wives and many children, as was the custom of the time. Joseph was the eleventh of Jacob's twelve sons. Joseph's mother, Rachel, died in childbirth giving birth to Benjamin, Joseph's younger brother.

Of his many wives, Jacob loved Rachel most of all. As the first born of his beloved Rachel, Jacob indulged Joseph considerably. Joseph was not expected to work alongside his brothers. Evidence of Joseph's privileged position was always on display in a coat Jacob gave Joseph to wear. With its many colors and flowing sleeves, it was suited only for pomp, not work. As one biblical scholar notes, Joseph's coat was a "tunic or robe unique in design for showing special favor or relationship" and that "either the robe was very long-sleeved and extending to the feet, or a richly ornamented tunic either of special color design or gold threading, both ornamental and not suitable for working."[48]

Jacob's partiality toward Joseph created considerable friction among Joseph's older half-brothers. As described in the verses below, one day when Joseph sauntered out wearing his flowing coat of many colors to view his brothers as they worked in the fields, they, in anger and resentment, beat him. They debated whether to kill him, ultimately agreeing to sell him to traders who were passing by on their way to Egypt. Joseph's brothers took the hated coat, soaked it in a goat's blood, and gave it to their father. They lied to their father about what had happened, telling Jacob that wild animals had attacked and killed Joseph:

"Joseph, being seventeen years old, was feeding the flock with his brothers. Now Jacob loved Joseph more than all his children, because he was the son of his old age. Jacob gave Joseph a tunic of many colors. When his brothers saw that their father loved him more than all his brothers, they hated him and could not speak peaceably to him.

"His brothers went to feed their father's flock in Shechem. Then Jacob said to Joseph, 'Please go and see if it is well with your brothers and well with the flocks and bring back word to me.' Now when the brothers saw Joseph in his tunic of many colors afar off, even before he came near them, they conspired against him to kill him. Then they said to one another, 'Look, the dreamer is coming! Come therefore, let us now kill him and cast him into some pit; and we shall say, 'Some wild beast has devoured him. We shall see what will become of his dreams!'

"So it came to pass, when Joseph had come to his brothers, that they stripped Joseph of his tunic, the tunic of many colors that was on him. Then they took him and cast him into a pit.

... And they sat down to eat a meal. Then they lifted their eyes and looked, and there was a company of Ishmaelites coming... bearing spices, balm, and myrrh, on their way to carry them down to Egypt. So Judah said to his brothers, 'What profit is there if we kill our brother and conceal his blood? Come and let us sell him to the Ishmaelites, and let not our hand be upon him, for he is our brother and our flesh.' And his brothers listened. So the brothers pulled Joseph up and lifted him out of the pit and sold him to the Ishmaelites for twenty shekels of silver. And the Ishmaelites took Joseph to Egypt."

Then they took Joseph's robe, slaughtered a goat, and dipped the robe in the blood. They had the long robe with sleeves taken to their father, and they said, 'This we have found; see now whether it is your son's robe or not.' He recognized it, and said, 'It is my son's robe! A wild animal has devoured him.' (Genesis 27:2-33)

When the traders arrived in Egypt, they sold Joseph to Potiphar, one of the Pharaoh's officials. For the first time in his life, Joseph had to work to survive. In doing so he discovered that he had abilities and skills he did not know he had because he had never been called upon to use them. He earned the trust of Potiphar who named Joseph as overseer of all of Potiphar's property (Genesis 39:2-4). Enamored by the handsome, good- looking Joseph, Potiphar's wife made advances towards Joseph which Joseph spurned (Genesis 39:6). Furious at Joseph's rejection and full of spite, Potiphar's wife told her husband that Joseph had attacked her. Potiphar, enraged, banished Joseph to prison (Genesis 39:19).

While in prison, Joseph again demonstrated the leadership he had shown when working for Potiphar. Recognizing his abilities, his jailers gave him considerable responsibility, "committing to Joseph's care all the prisoners" (Genesis 39:22). Joseph showed kindness to his fellow prisoners, listening to their troubles and helping them interpret their dreams (Genesis 40: 6-7). One of these prisoners was a man who had been the Pharaoh's "cupbearer" before he went to prison. After a period of time the cupbearer was released from prison and was reemployed by the Pharaoh (Genesis14). When the Pharaoh began having disturbing dreams that no one could interpret, the cupbearer, recalling Joseph's ability to interpret dreams, suggested to the Pharaoh that Joseph may be able to interpret his dreams.

The Pharaoh called for Joseph's release from prison and told him of his dreams. Joseph interpreted the Pharaoh's dreams as foreshadowing seven years of good harvest followed by seven years of famine. Joseph suggested that Egypt should harvest the surplus grain during the years of plenty, store it, and save it for the years of famine (Genesis 41:33). Grain storage was a novel concept at that time. Neither storage silos nor mechanisms for trading or transporting grain existed but Joseph suggested how a system of grain storage could be built. Impressed by Joseph's creative and practical suggestions, the Pharaoh appointed Joseph as overseer of a nation-wide grain storage program for Egypt.

As Joseph had predicted, Egypt experienced seven years of plentiful harvest followed by seven years of drought. Because of the storage program Joseph had established, Egypt had enough grain to feed Egyptians as well as to trade with neighboring nations, one of which was Canaan, Joseph's birthplace. Canaan, like many nations in the area, had been devastated by years of drought. Joseph's family, like all Canaanites, was desperate for food. Jacob, still the family patriarch, sent his sons to Egypt to trade for food.

Never suspecting that their younger brother was now an esteemed and powerful person in Egypt, Joseph's brothers did not recognize Joseph when they were brought before him with their request for grain. Joseph made himself known to his brothers who "threw themselves down before him," exclaiming "we are your slaves" (Genesis 50: 18). Joseph spoke kindly to his brothers: "You intended to harm me, but God intended it for good to accomplish what is now being done, the saving of many lives. So then, do not be afraid. I will provide for you and your children" (Genesis 50:19-21).

As this story shows, Joseph learned to face adversity and developed into a remarkably resilient person. With each difficulty, Joseph grew from a spoiled youth to a loyal employee, friend, wise leader, and finally, truly in God's image, a person able to extend grace and forgiveness.

Behavioral Science Of Resilience

Behavioral scientists define resilience as the ability to bounce back after difficulty. The American Psychological Association defines resilience as "the process of adapting well in the face of adversity, trauma, tragedy, threats and significant sources of stress — such as family and relational problems, serious health problems, or workplace and financial stresses."[49] Studies show that while individuals may demonstrate resilience in some domains of their life, they may not in all. A person may be quite competent at handling setbacks in his or her professional life, for example, but not as much in personal or family life. Studies show that people often become more resilient as they go through life, becoming better able to weather difficulties as they grow older, life slows down, or they have more time for things they enjoy. For others, the opposite is true.

Steven M. Southwick, MD, professor of psychiatry at Yale University Medical School, and Dennis S. Charney, MD, professor of psychiatry, neuroscience and pharmacology at Mount Sinai School of Medicine, studied resilience by studying thousands of individuals who lived through trauma including combat, child abuse, physical assault, sexual assault, bombings, and natural disasters.[50]

Drs Southwick and Charney began multi-year studies of resilient individuals by conducting lengthy interviews with former prisoners of war during the Vietnam War of the 1960s and 1970s. One reason they chose to study this group was that decades had passed since their imprisonment, and they would be able to observe how the differences in the ways these former POWs handled their years of imprisonment impacted their lives after their release.

Southwick and Carney also studied special forces instructors in the US Army. These individuals participated in highly stressful missions of war and humanitarian rescues. They also received constant training in principles and techniques of resilience. Southwick and Carney wanted to see if this training impacted these individuals' lifelong ability to bounce back from adversity.

Lastly, Southwick and Carney interviewed civilians who went on to live full and productive lives after experiencing significant trauma such as congenital medical problems, childhood sexual abuse, death of parents at an early age, abductions and rape, loss of a limb, or cancer.

The questions Drs. Southwick and Carney explored in these studies were: Are there common characteristics among those who had demonstrated resilience compared to those who did not? Did the resilient individuals carry forth resilience throughout life? What are the skills of resilience? From their studies, Southwick and Carney found "recurrent themes." As they summarize: "Although their circumstances differed greatly, the resilient people we interviewed tended to use the same or similar coping strategies."

The strategies of resilience Southwick and Carney identified are: 1) a sense of optimism, 2) an ability to face fear, 3) maintaining a moral compass, 4) drawing on faith, religion, spirituality, 5) having social support, 6) available role models of emotionally healthy individuals, 7) maintaining physical fitness, 8) maintaining "brain fitness, 9) cognitive and emotional stability, 10) having a sense of meaning and purpose. All of these strategies are listed and briefly summarized in the appendix to this chapter. We focus on three of these strategies in this chapter's discussion: realistic optimism, altruism, and faith.

- *Realistic Optimism*: Optimism is the ability to see the good in situations we face. Excessive or unrealistic optimism is not healthy, because it can lead to an "optimist's bias," where one underestimates risk, overestimates ability, and inadequately prepares. "Realistic optimism" is balancing optimism with an accurate perception of reality. A realistic optimist is able to see the good in situations while paying attention to and preparing for upsetting and unpleasant eventualities without becoming overwhelmed by those. As Southwick and Carney explain:

    "[R]ealistic optimists pay close attention to negative information that is relevant to the problems they face. However, unlike pessimists, they do not remain focused on the negative. They tend to disengage rapidly from problems that appear to be unsolvable. That is, they know when to cut their losses and turn their attention to problems that they believe they can solve."[51]

- *Altruism*: According to Southwick and Carney, altruism, another resiliency strategy, is "associated with resilience, positive mental health and wellbeing."[52] It "enhances self-confidence and self-acceptance, reframes one's own experience and provides greater meaning in life."[53] Southwick and Charney explain:

> "Altruism, or what some call social interest, is associated with better life adjustment, better marital adjustment and less hopelessness and depression. Receiving help from others and giving help to others both predicted better mental health, although giving help to others was a strong predictor."[54]

Simply put, altruism is helping others. Helping others *helps us* because of what it gives us: perspective that our situations are not as bad as we thought, and a better ability to get outside of ourselves and stop focusing so much on our own problems. Functional brain imaging (FMRI) shows that helping others actually leads to biological changes generating the release of hormones and changes in our brains that calm and uplift us.

How does helping others provide perspective? When we provide food to the poor or sick, hold a door for someone who is wheelchair bound, or visit a friend in the hospital, we are granted a glimpse into the life of someone who has things harder than we do. This gives us a gift, if we choose to see it, of gratitude for what we have. This is aptly demonstrated in the following story:

> *"Last summer, I moved into an apartment building. After my husband died, I have often felt so lonely, it seemed my heart was on fire with so much sadness. It is so easy to feel lonely and a little sorry for myself. I knew I could end up isolating myself in that little apartment. So I decided to get to know a few of my neighbors.*
>
> *"I met Marie, who lives just across the hall. She is confined to a wheelchair; she has cerebral palsy.*
>
> *"I started to go over every once in a while. It was hard for Marie to cook from her wheelchair, so I would bring over food I had made. Some nights I would even stay and eat with her. It*

was good for both of us to feel some companionship in the big city.

"One night we got to talking about our husbands and our children, and we lost track of the time. As I was leaving, a little later than usual, I asked Marie if there was anything she needed before I went back to my apartment.

"She didn't answer right away. I think she felt awkward about asking. But then she said, "Every night, before I go to sleep, I have to take off my braces, and then my shoes, and then my socks. If I do it by myself, it takes me about an hour. At night when I am tired, I have to stop every ten minutes or so to rest. But it's so hard to get a good night's sleep if I don't take them off." Marie paused, a little embarrassed by her confession. "I don't like to ask, but if you wouldn't mind taking off my braces for me, I would get to sleep so much easier."

"Now it was my turn to feel awkward. I didn't know what to say. It was such a simple thing; it had never occurred to me to ask about Marie's legs. Like most people, I am a little uncomfortable when people have a disability. I don't want to ask the wrong question or seem insensitive. When I don't know the right thing to say or ask, I usually say nothing at all.

"Of course, I agreed, and it took me only a few minutes to do what Marie had to do every night, alone for over an hour. I took off each brace, and then each shoe and sock, and put them by the bed for Marie to put on the next morning. Marie had tears in her eyes, I think I did too.

"No one has helped me do this for a very long time," she shared. "Not since my husband passed away. Now, tonight I can get a good, long sleep. Thank you so much." I put my hand on hers. I may have whispered a little prayer for her, maybe for both of us, and then I went home.

"I realized I suddenly felt so very grateful for everything in my life."[55]

- *Faith, Spirituality*: All of the resilient individuals studied had a strong sense of faith. As Southwick and Charney summarize: "In our interviews with highly resilient individuals, time and again we were told about the powerful effects of spirituality or religion." [56]

Interviews with survivors of a devastating earthquake in Pakistan, for example, showed "religious belief among survivors to be the single most powerful force in explaining the tragedy and in explaining survival."[57] Interviews with American prisoners of war held during the Vietnam War, showed, "there is virtually no personal account in the Vietnam POW literature that does not contain some reference to a transforming spiritual episode."[58] Indeed, the advice one American POW always gave to new POWs coming into the Vietcong prison was: "The first thing you need around here, old buddy, is faith. I'm not a preacher. I'm not gonna try to convert you. I'm just gonna tell you the truth. If you can't tap into a source of strength and power greater than yourself, you're probably not gonna last."[59]

Meta-analyses of numerous research studies confirm Southwick and Charney's findings about the strength of faith. Spiritual practices are associated with longer life,[60] better health,[61] fewer hospital stays,[62] and lower levels of depression.[63]

Having looked at these three strategies of resilient individuals, let us now turn to Liz Huntley, who as a young girl living in tragic circumstances heard about Joseph and decided that if Joseph could overcome the setbacks he faced, so could she.

Liz

Liz Huntley was five years old when her mother, a drug addict and drug dealer, committed suicide. Liz's father, newly released from prison for dealing drugs, was unable to care for Liz and her siblings. Liz and one of her sisters were sent to live with their grandmother in a housing project in Clanton, Alabama.

Two of Liz's uncles, Uncle John and Uncle Tim, also lived in her grandmother's home. One afternoon when no one else was home, Uncle John commanded Liz to do as he instructed. If she did not, he threatened, he would kill Liz and her sister in their sleep and if Liz told anyone what he was doing to her Liz and her sister would have to move out. From that moment on, Liz's life "as a child was over."[64]

Uncle Tim, who also lived in the home, was a paranoid schizophrenic whose behavior often became uncontrollable. He would fly into rages and throw things or grab a butcher knife and threaten to kill everyone. Sometimes the neighbors would call the police who would take Uncle Tim into custody for a few days. At these times, Liz felt relief: "Although I hurt for my grandma and I dreaded how the kids might make fun of my situation the following day at school, that night, I slept like a baby. I had no Uncle Tim to worry about."

When Liz was eight years old, an aunt invited her to go to church. Liz went to church regularly with her grandmother "but never got much out it." Her aunt's church was different, however. The day Liz visited with her aunt, the sermon was about Joseph and "how God used Joseph's life in spite of all of its tragic events." After hearing about Joseph's life, Liz thought to herself, "If God can use Joseph's life for good even though all of those bad things happened to him, maybe he can use my life." As Liz describes, "When I walked into that church, I felt like a used rag doll. I was so depressed; I was on the verge of suicide. When I left that church, for the first time in my life, I felt hope for my future."

From that moment on, Liz began to see as she puts it, "the opportunities and resources God was placing in my life." In her book, *More Than a Bird*, Liz described those resources. One was the preschool close to the housing project where Liz lived. Liz loved going there. Others were her teachers: the loving first grade teacher who recognized Liz's potential and nurtured it; the teacher who arranged for Liz to get speech therapy; the teacher who introduced Liz to challenging books and courses; the teacher who gave Liz rides to extracurricular activities; the teacher who provided Liz with early morning access to the school computer lab; the multiple teachers who helped Liz apply for college scholarships. Another was the pastor who had preached the sermon about Joseph and who, with his family, welcomed Liz into their home when Liz's grandmother became too sick to care for her. As Liz says, with each person "God was providing the resources needed for me to achieve a goal."

Liz graduated from high school as valedictorian and attended college and law school on scholarships. She married her college sweetheart; they are parents of three beautiful children. Today, Liz practices law with a nationally known law firm, and is co-founder of the Hope Institute of Samford University which offers curricula on character for high school teachers. She is a nationally known advocate for preschool education.

The Ties That Bind: Resilience In Day-To-Day Life

Note how Joseph and Liz, both incredibly resilient, were realistic optimists. When sold into slavery and transported to a foreign country, Joseph had to face the painful fact of his new situation before he could discover and begin to use talents he did not know he had. No longer was Joseph the beloved son of a wealthy landowner but a slave in a foreign land. When Joseph was falsely accused of wrongdoing and sent to prison he had to face the disappointing reality that he had lost all he had gained in his new life. Only then could he begin to make the best of his new circumstances in prison, which he did by befriending others and helping the jailers. By looking past his disappointments and continuing to grow as a person, Joseph ended up helping himself by his willingness to listen to the stories, fears, and dreams of his fellow prisoners.

Likewise, Liz did not sugarcoat, deny, or ignore the horrific abuse she suffered at her grandmother's home, but neither did she let those deeds define her as a victim or stop her from achieving all she could. As Liz said, "I learned that even if a person is born into terrible circumstances like I was, God can provide the resources needed for success." Liz took advantage of the resources she found in her path. She excelled in school, which led her out of the tragic life she had.

Note also how both Joseph's and Liz's lives epitomize altruism. Thrust unfairly into prison, Joseph helped his jailers with their work and helped his fellow prisoners by listening to them and interpreting their dreams. Once freed from prison, Joseph used his abilities to help Egypt and surrounding nations survive a drought. When he met his brothers, he helped them by giving them food, and through his forgiveness, dignity.

Liz has demonstrated unparalleled altruism. While a full-time law student, Liz established and ran Project GEAR, a tutoring and mentoring program for at risk youth in her hometown, Clanton, Alabama. Today, Liz, in addition to being a wife, mother of three children, and a highly recognized attorney, is a tireless advocate for character education and preschool education. Her efforts have resulted in hundreds of programs being offered in Alabama and throughout the United States for young children. With a former Alabama Supreme Court chief justice, Liz founded the HOPE Institute at Samford University which provides curricula, speakers, and programs on character for high school youth.

Note lastly, how their faith was the source of strength for Joseph and for Liz. When Joseph was sold into slavery and transported to a different land, we are told, *"The Lord was with Joseph."* (Genesis 38.4) When he was sold to Potiphar (Genesis 39:2), Potiphar *"saw that the Lord was with Joseph"* (Genesis 39:3). When Potiphar's wife *"cast her eyes upon Joseph,"* Joseph refused her, saying, *"How could I do this great wickedness and sin against God?"* (Genesis 39:9). When he was thrown into prison, *"the Lord was with Joseph and showed him steadfast love..."* (Genesis 39:21). When Joseph was brought *"out of the dungeon"* to the Pharaoh and commanded to interpret the Pharaoh's dream, Joseph responded, *"It is not I; God will interpret your dream."* (Genesis 41:16). When he revealed himself to his brothers and forgave them for selling him into slavery, Joseph felt God at work in him, saying to his brothers, *"And now do not be distressed, or angry with yourselves, because you sold me here; for God sent me before you to preserve life."* (Genesis 45:4-8) Throughout his life as challenges arose, Joseph's constant was seeing God's hand reaching to him through the people he encountered and opportunities available.

As a child in Clanton, Alabama, Liz heard God speaking to her through the story of Joseph. From that point on, she saw God helping her every step of the way, through the people and opportunities available to her. As Liz said, "God showed me a loving humanity that transcended racial divides and overcame the obstacles of a segregated community and pitfalls of an integrated school. I will forever be grateful for the way God used my community and all the people around me to change the course of my life."

Conclusion

Both Joseph and Liz demonstrated resilience in facing the challenges and setbacks that came their way, exemplifying three resiliency traits. Both were *realistic optimists* in assessing the difficulties and problems they faced while also focusing on, and making the most of, the opportunities and resources available to them. Both demonstrated how *helping others* gives strength and perspective. Joseph helped his fellow prisoners by listening to them with kindness and wisdom. He helped the people of Egypt and surrounding nations by devising grain storage systems. He helped his brothers by forgiving them. Liz lives a life of service, passing along to young people the gifts of mentoring, education, and hope that others gave her. For both, *faith* has been the bedrock of their ability to overcome and grow from setbacks. Joseph and Liz serve as powerful examples of resilience.

Resilience is one of the most important emotional intelligence skills we can develop because we all will need it. Whoever we are and whatever our circumstances, one guarantee in life is that we will encounter adversities, setbacks, and difficulties. With resilience we too can make it through these valleys of life and live fuller, happier, more productive, healthier lives, and more into the image of God.

Questions For Thought And Reflection

1. What are some of the challenges you have faced in your life? What are the resources God has provided to you in facing these challenges?

2. How have you grown as a result of the adversities you've faced?

3. Both Joseph and Liz benefitted from the help of others. Who are some of the people who have helped you overcome adversities? How can you serve as God's hands and feet?

4. What do you think was the most difficult challenge Joseph confronted? Having his life upended when he was sold into slavery? Being falsely accused and imprisoned? Forgiving his brothers? What resources did God provide to Joseph throughout each of these challenges and how did Joseph make the best of them? What was the most difficult challenge Liz faced: Uncle John? Uncle Tim? Being raised in poverty? What resources did God provide for Liz?

5. This chapter has discussed three of the ten "resilience traits" behavioral scientists have identified as characteristic of resilient individuals. All ten are listed and summarized in the appendix to this chapter. What do you think of this list? Which do you have? Which do you wish you had or had more of? What steps can you take to develop your resiliency traits?

Appendix To Chapter Four: The Ten Factors Of Resilience[65]

1. *Optimism: Belief in a Bright Future.* "Optimism is a future-oriented attitude, involving hope and confidence that things will turn out well. Optimists believe that the future will be bright, that good things will happen to them, and that with enough hard work they will succeed." Resilience requires being a realistic optimist which is "paying close attention to negative information that is relevant to the problems one faces...[Un]like pessimists," realistic optimists do not remain focused on the negative. They tend to disengage rapidly from problems that appear to be unsolvable. That is, they know when to cut their losses and turn their attention to problems that they believe they can solve."[66]

2. *Facing Fear: An Adaptive Response.* "To become more resilient, sooner or later we will need to face our fears." There are multiple ways to face one's fears, including "extended exposure to moderate or strong fear-producing cues,"[67] eye movement desensitization and reprocessing therapy (EMDR),[68] cognitive pressing therapy (CPT),[69] helping one understand when and why various fear- conditioned stimuli make one feel anxious and afraid,[70] understanding the difference between fear and panic, "focus on the goal or mission, acquire information about what is feared, learn and practice the skills necessary to master the fear, face fear with friends or colleagues, face fear with spiritual support, get someone or an organization to push you."[71]

3. *Moral Compass, Ethics, and Altruism: Doing What is Right.* In their interviews with resilient individuals, Southwick and Carney "found that many resilient individuals possessed a keen sense of right and wrong that strengthened them during periods of extreme stress and afterward...Also altruism — selflessness, concern for the welfare of others, and giving to others with no expectation of benefit to the self — often stood as a pillar of their value system, of their 'moral compass.'"[72]

4. *Religion and Spirituality, Drawing on Faith.* As discussed in this chapter, whether interviewing survivors of natural disasters such as earthquakes, horrific accidents, or POWs, researchers have found that "religious belief among survivors to be the single most

powerful force in explain the tragedy and in explaining survival." In Southwick and Charney's interviews with "highly resilient individuals, time and again we were told about the powerful effects of spirituality or religion, particularly during times of high stress."[73] Chapter Five of Southwick and Charney's book on their research details biological and physical advantages of religion, spirituality and prayer.[74]

5. *Social Support.* As Southwick and Charney said, "In order to thrive in this world, people need other people. We all benefit by knowing that someone cares about our welfare and will support us if we fall. Even better is having an entire network of family and close friends who will come to our aid at a moment's notice. It is also important for us to give of ourselves to help others. Forming relationships may not seem important when times are good, when we tend to take our friends and family for granted. However, close relationships build strength and help to protect us during times of stress and danger. Far from signifying weakness, interdependence with others can provide a foundation for resilience."[75]

6. *Role Models: Providing the Road Map.* Researchers of resilient children found that "the ones who grew up to be productive, emotionally healthy adults had at least one person in their lives who truly supported them and served as an admired role model." Southwick and Carney's study of resilient adults showed "a similar pattern." All of the resilient individuals they interviewed had "role models whose beliefs, attitudes and behaviors inspire them."[76] Effective role models can be parents, teachers, a friend and peer, even "famous athletes, political leaders, historical figures, even fictional characters from literature."[77]

7. *Training: Physical fitness and Strengthening.* Physical training, proper nutrition, and adequate sleep not only enhances general health and reduces the likelihood of many debilitating conditions, but it also improves mood, cognition and emotional resilience.[78] Importantly, as discussed in chapter eight of this book, healthy physical habits increase key hormones we need to manage stress.

8. *Brain Fitness: Challenge Your Mind and Heart.* Resilient people "tend to be mentally sharp" which helps them "focus on the problem, process information quickly, find strategies to solve problems, make wise decisions, learn new information, recover from setbacks."[79] Brain fitness includes the ability to regulate one's emotions, as discussed in chapter seven of this book.

9. *Cognitive and Emotional Flexibility.* According to Southwick and Carney, "People who are resilient tend to be flexible...in the way they think about challenges and flexible in the way they react emotionally to stress. They are not wedded to a specific style of coping. Instead, they shift from one coping strategy to another depending on the circumstances. Many are able to accept what they cannot change; to learn from failure, to use emotions like grief and anger to fuel compassion and courage; and to search for opportunity and meaning in adversity."[80]

10. *Meaning, Purpose, and Growth.* Studies of resilient individuals show that "having a clear and valued purpose...can dramatically strengthen one's resilience."[81] Notably, these studies affirm what philosophers ranging from Frederick Nietzsche ("He who has a why can endure almost any how.")[82] to Victor Frankl ("Man is dominated neither by the will to pleasure nor by the will to power but a deep-seeded desire for higher and ultimate meaning.")[83] to the Bible *"He has told you what is good; and what does the Lord require of you but to do justice, and to love kindness, and to walk humbly with your God?"* (Micah 6:8)

CHAPTER FIVE: EMOTIONAL STABILITY: MANAGING OUR EMOTIONAL TEMPERAMENT

This chapter addresses emotional stability which is maintaining stability throughout the ups and downs of life. While we are all born with an innate temperament, biology is not our destiny. Our temperament is shaped by emotional lessons we learn throughout life, whether from parents, friends, or experiences. This chapter focuses on the story of Peter, one of the more volatile people in the Bible, and on Alyce Manley Spruell, who experienced chaos while growing up because her beloved mother was an alcoholic. We see how lessons of emotional intelligence, taught by Jesus to Peter, and by a loving family and church community to Alyce, chart the way for all of us to grow into emotional stability.

Peter
Peter, a fisherman, accepted Jesus's invitation to become a disciple after witnessing Jesus's abilities.

> "So it was, as the multitude pressed about him to hear the word of God, that he stood by the Lake of Gennesaret, and saw two boats standing by the lake; but the fishermen had gone from them and were washing their nets. Then he got into one of the boats, which was Simon's, and asked him to put out a little from the land. And he sat down and taught the multitudes from the boat.
>
> "When he had stopped speaking, he said to Simon, 'Launch out into the deep and let down your nets for a catch.' But Simon answered and said to him, 'Master, we have toiled all night and caught nothing; nevertheless, at your word I will let down the net.'
>
> "And when they had done this, they caught a great number of fish, and their net was breaking. So they signaled to their partners in the other boat to come and help them. And they came and filled both the boats, so that they began to sink. When Simon Peter saw it, he fell down at Jesus' knees, saying, 'Depart from me, for I am a sinful man, O Lord!'

> "For he and all who were with him were astonished at the catch of fish which they had taken; and so also were James and John, the sons of Zebedee, who were partners with Simon. And Jesus said to Simon, 'Do not be afraid. From now on you will catch men.' So when they had brought their boats to land, they forsook all and followed him." Luke 5:1-11.

Peter vacillated from disbelief to obedience, from astonishment to belief, from terror to boldness, from fear to radical trust and adoration, all in a matter of minutes.

> "When the disciples saw (Jesus) walking on the lake, they were terrified. 'It's a ghost,' they said, and cried out in fear. But Jesus immediately said to them: 'Take courage! It is I. Don't be afraid.' 'LORD, if it's you,' Peter replied, 'tell me to come to you on the water.' 'Come,' he said. Then Peter got down out of the boat, walked on the water and came toward Jesus. But when he saw the wind, he was afraid and, beginning to sink, cried out, 'LORD, save me!' Immediately Jesus reached out his hand and caught him. 'You of little faith,' he said, 'why did you doubt?' And when they climbed into the boat, the wind died down. Then those who were in the boat worshiped him, saying, 'Truly you are the Son of God.'" (Matthew 14:26-33)

Even after the resurrection, Peter still acted on impulse and needed instruction from his Lord. Within minutes, Peter once again vacillated rapidly between obtuseness to boldness to impulsive action to sadness to a new level of belief.

> "Afterward Jesus appeared again to his disciples, by the Sea of Galilee. It happened this way: Simon Peter, Thomas (also known as Didymus), Nathanael from Cana in Galilee, the sons of Zebedee, and two other disciples were together. 'I'm going out to fish,' Simon Peter told them, and they said, 'We'll go with you.'
>
> So they went out and got into the boat, but that night they caught nothing.
>
> "Early in the morning, Jesus stood on the shore, but the disciples did not realize that it was Jesus. He called out to them, 'Friends, haven't you any fish?' 'No,' they answered. He said, 'Throw your net on the right side of the boat and you will find some.' When they did, they were unable to haul the net in because of the large number of fish.

> "Then the disciple whom Jesus loved said to Peter, 'It is the Lord!' As soon as Simon Peter heard him say, 'It is the Lord,' he wrapped his outer garment around him (for he had taken it off) and jumped into the water. The other disciples followed in the boat, towing the net full of fish, for they were not far from shore, about a hundred yards. When they landed, they saw a fire of burning coals there with fish on it, and some bread. Jesus said to them, 'Bring some of the fish you have just caught.'
>
> "So Simon Peter climbed back into the boat and dragged the net ashore. It was full of large fish, but even with so many the net was not torn. Jesus said to them, 'Come and have breakfast.' None of the disciples dared ask him, 'Who are you?' They knew it was the Lord. Jesus came, took the bread and gave it to them, and did the same with the fish.
>
> "This was now the third time Jesus appeared to his disciples after he was raised from the dead. When they had finished eating, Jesus said to Simon Peter, 'Simon son of John, do you love me more than these?' 'Yes, Lord,' he said, 'you know that I love you.' Jesus said, 'Feed my lambs.'
>
> "Again, Jesus said, 'Simon, son of John, do you love me?' He answered, 'Yes, Lord, you know that I love you.' Jesus said, 'Take care of my sheep.' The third time he said to him, 'Simon son of John, do you love me?' Peter was hurt because Jesus asked him the third time, Do you love me? He said, 'Lord, you know all things; you know that I love you.' Jesus said, 'Feed my sheep.'" (John 21: 1-17).

No biblical figure is more temperamental than Peter, who often showed his choleric nature. We saw three examples of Jesus's patience helping the impetuous Peter discipline his temperamental nature. Undoubtedly, there are countless more examples of Jesus's patience helping Peter and others learn to channel their emotions into constructive actions. As John said at the end of his gospel, "And there are also many other things which Jesus did, which, if they should be written, I suppose that even the world itself could not contain the books that should be written." (John 21:25)

Did Jesus provide the parenting Peter may have missed earlier in his life? Or perhaps was Jesus, the original psychotherapist, providing Peter with "systematic emotional relearning"? Did Jesus help Peter tame his impulsivity, passion, and fear when he gave him a new direction in life: "From now on you will catch men." When Jesus "reached out his hand and caught Peter" saying "Do not be afraid," when Peter, terrified, began to sink in the water? When Jesus, appearing for the third and last time to his disciples after his resurrection, asked Peter, three times, "Simon, son of John, do you love me" and each time, guided Peter toward a new direction in life: "Feed my lambs." "Take care of my sheep." "Feed my sheep." (John 21: 1-17).

Wise parenting, as Jesus gave to Peter, has been proven to tame temperament. Patience and consistency in allowing Peter to meet the unexpected in life and to learn better ways of dealing with it were keys to rewiring the temperamental brain. Jesus certainly gave Peter ample opportunity to make mistakes over and over, and eventually Peter was transformed.

Thankfully, Jesus never gave up on Peter, despite his running hot and cold. He often kept Peter especially close to him, exactly what Peter needed to keep balance in his life. Jesus had confidence that Peter would be able to "strengthen his brothers" even after his failures (Luke 22:31-32). Jesus's final words to Peter were "Follow me." (John 21:17). As Peter followed Christ, keeping always close to him, the weakness of his temperament could be transformed by his passion for his Lord's work. That is how he would keep his impulsive nature in check.

Jesus knew this over two thousand years ago. His persistence and patience with Peter, and Peter's staying close to Jesus before and after the resurrection, changed Peter from an impulsive follower to a strong and courageous leader.

Behavioral Science On Emotional Stability

Temperament is generally defined as "the moods that typify our emotional life."[84] In one sense, "temperament is a given at birth, part of the genetic lottery that has compelling force in the unfolding of life,"[85] and in fact, behavioral scientists have identified four general types of temperament: timid, bold, upbeat, and melancholy. To an extent, these temperaments are hard-wired. Each type shows a different level of "excitability in the neural circuitry of the amygdala," an almond-shaped mass located deep within the temporal lobes of the brain. The amygdala of individuals who tend to be timid, for example, is easily aroused when these individuals face new situations or meet new people, or otherwise become fearful. By contrast, the amygdala of those individuals who tend to be bold or upbeat show less neural activity when they meet new people, explore new places, and seek out new experiences.[86]

The encouraging news from behavioral science is that "temperament is not destiny."[87] Our emotional temperament can change. We can change our amygdala patterns and our resulting emotional patterns by developing self-awareness, [88] self-regulation[89] and other healthy emotional habits.

A study by L.R. Baxter, for example, demonstrates that patients with obsessive-compulsive disorder have the same symptom relief and change in brain function with behavior therapy as with successful medication, showing that in fact, "emotional habits are malleable throughout life, with some sustained effort, even at the neural level."[90] Daniel Goleman's research affirms that re-shaping neural patterns in the brain can change our emotional temperament. For example, "one of the most essential emotional lessons, first learned in infancy and refined throughout childhood, is how to soothe oneself when upset."[91]

Wise parenting and modeling (or, for those who may not have had wise parenting, by parent figures, wise friends, or other role models) can change our emotional destiny. Emotional lessons throughout life, especially during childhood and puberty, can, for example, transform the timid child into an outgoing and calm person when encountering new situations. The critical emotional lessons children need "include how dependable and responsive to the children's needs parents are, the opportunities and guidance a child has in learning to handle her own distress and control impulse, and practice in empathy."[92] For those who may not have obtained lessons in managing emotions and temperament while growing up, "systematic emotional relearning stands as a case in point for the way experience can both change emotional patterns and shape the brain." [93]

Alyce

"I had an outstanding mother and father," Alyce Manley Spruell says with a huge smile. "Mom was the first head of the Alabama Commission on Higher Education, a remarkable achievement for a woman at the time. Ironically, she had just lost the presidency of Judson College (an all-female Baptist college) to a man."

When Alyce was fourteen, during the summer before her freshman year in high school, she "started to notice Mom acting weird." Alyce's father had told her early in her life that she "had the ears of an elephant," always listening and noticing. "I guess my elephant ears were working that summer," Alyce says. One evening, in the spring of her freshman year, when her father came home from work, Alyce said to him, "Mom's not acting right. She tells me to leave her alone."

Alyce's dad said, "I'll handle this, darling. She's dealing with stuff." Alyce knew her mother's family dynamics were difficult at that time. Her maternal grandfather, her mother's father, had recently passed away. Alyce knew that her mother was especially close to her father, and not to her mother. Alyce's maternal grandmother, who had no more than a fourth-grade education but had been successful in business, had wanted her daughter to go into business instead of education. Thereafter Alyce's mom and her mother did not have a close relationship. All of these family dynamics seemed a plausible explanation for her mother's behavior, but Alyce was still worried. She said, "Dad, you've got to take Mom to the hospital."

At that point, Alyce's brother, Dick, who was three years older than Alyce, said to their father, "You've got to tell her." Dick and Alyce's dad had protected Alyce as long as they could from the truth of her mother's disease. Alyce was totally shocked to learn that her mother was an alcoholic.

Alyce's mom continued to decline as more family changes occurred. Dick's recent college decision to attend Vanderbilt University, "horrified' their mother who had always wanted her children, like herself and their father, to go to the University of Alabama. When Dick received a scholarship from Vanderbilt and committed to go there, their mother "went off the deep end." Meanwhile, Alyce's father, a practicing attorney and elected member of the Alabama legislature, had been appointed as the Birmingham Commandant of the Marine Corps Reserves, which meant he traveled a lot, especially to Kentucky and Louisiana. United States Marine Corps Reserves Battalion for the Birmingham region , which meant he traveled a lot to other states that were part of that unit. The upshot of all of these changes meant that Alyce "assumed much responsibility for mom."

The chaos got worse. As Alyce explained: "Over the next couple of months, I began to notice my parents fighting at home. Then, one of the first public episodes of mom's drunkenness occurred at the very beginning of sophomore year. I had become a cheerleader. Mom had committed to drive a group of us to the first football game at an out of town location. Dad was scheduled to meet us at the game, but I observed that mom was too drunk to drive. She became combative when I confronted her and cussed like a sailor."

"So, I hid all the alcohol in the attic and called a friend to drive because 'Mom has a migraine.' While we were gone, mom frantically searched for alcohol. In the process, she locked herself out of the house and then used a hatchet to get in the back door. I returned home after the game with Dad and two friends to spend the night to find the back door handle totally destroyed.. Dad and I explained that some robbers had tried to get in the house."

"Another episode had occurred during the summer when I was working as a lifeguard at the country club down the street from our house and observed my mom walking down the street in a swimsuit carrying a beach towel and a suitcase. Dad had taken all of the alcohol out of our home, and mom decided to walk to the country club to get a drink. I grabbed a friend to replace me on the lifeguard stand and took her home.

"That same summer, I received a call from a local gas station manager to come get mom because she was drunk and trying to buy beer. Although I was only fifteen and only had a learners permit, I drove there and brought her home. That was not the only time before I was sixteen and licensed to drive that I had to drive to rescue mom or drive myself to my other jobs at the local pharmacy and a bank. "In her public position as head of the Alabama Commission of Higher Education, others began to notice. The president of the University of Alabama, David Mathews, among others reached out to my father, saying 'You have to do something.'

"I was not going to leave Mom, so I decided in my senior year to attend the University of Alabama, even though I really wanted to go to Vandy and be there with my brother, but Dad and two of my wonderful teachers applied to Vanderbilt for me, and when I was accepted, I finally decided to go. I told Mom two weeks before she died.

"By then, mom was living in an apartment near our home. In March of my high school senior year, after a Sunday church service, I left with our Interact and Key Club group on a service project in Selma, but was stopped by my Mom's secretary and her husband went to Mom's apartment to check on her and found her dead from aspiration while intoxicated. The hardest thing I have ever had to do was locate Dad in an airport and and tell him that Mom had died, knowing he would hen call my brother, Dick, to tell him too.

The Ties That Bind: Emotional Stability In Day-to-Day Life
The "tie that binds" Peter's and Alyce's lives is God's presence. The faith Jesus taught Peter transformed Peter's emotional volatility. The faith Alyce's father and her church taught her transformed Alyce's childhood chaos. Their faith allowed both Peter and Alyce to become strong, compassionate leaders.

Peter's life is a beautiful example of how we can receive wise "parenting" at any age. Jesus's persistence and patience with Peter, and Peter's staying close to Jesus before and after the resurrection, changed Peter from an impulsive follower to a strong and courageous leader. Jesus's patience and consistency in allowing Peter to meet the unexpected in life and to learn better ways of dealing with it were keys to rewiring Peter's temperamental brain. Jesus certainly gave Peter ample opportunity to make mistakes over and over, and eventually Peter was transformed. Jesus's "parenting" of Peter is wise role modeling for all parents. Peter's passion and his inability to rein in his tempestuousness was used by God for good. One of the most convincing proofs of the power of Christ's resurrection and the mighty working of the Holy Spirit is the miraculous transformation of this temperamental fisherman into the rock on which the church was built.

How striking is "the contrast between the Peter of the gospels — impulsive, unsteadfast, slow of heart to understand the mysteries of the kingdom — and the same apostle as he meets us in the Acts — firm and courageous, ready to go to prison and to death, the preacher of the faith, the interpreter of scripture."[94] Equally marvelous is that none of Peter's characteristic passion is lost in his transformation to stability. That passion was redirected to be what God had created him to be: a strong, passionate leader of the church. In the same way, our God-given temperaments await transformation and redirection to stability.

We saw how from a young age, Alyce remained amazingly stable in a life of turmoil and chaos, which she attributes to her strong father, her church, and She said:

> *"I am so grateful to my father for teaching me to be a good listener. He also taught me that we can't know what life will bring, but we have to have faith that we are in God's hands and that he has a plan. Dad was always there for me and taught me that the Lord has blessed us with the ability to choose. I could choose to be angry, bitter, unhappy, or choose to look for the Lord's blessings. In dealing with life's inevitable troubles, we can choose to believe,*

> *have faith, and trust in the Lord. We also can choose to serve others, our purpose and the source of our happiness. If we serve others, we witness to the Lord and follow his path. And we cannot escape gratitude if we serve others in need. Experiencing that I could help Mom as a young person was a lightbulb experience for me."*

Alyce's family was active in her church, which she also relied upon during the hard and scary times: "I do not know what I would have done without the support of the Friday prayer group meeting before school at a teacher's home or my church youth group or the choir. But I almost dropped out because Mom came to church drunk on a couple of occasions during my high school years. Thank God, the director of the choir and my Dad refused to let me quit. My church leaders invested and poured so much into all of us. Church was a place of refuge and peace for me. I remember vividly in the second grade at church, hearing the Lord's Prayer as if for the first time. It touched my heart and was the first time that I 'got it.'"

Like Peter, Alyce's faith held her up. "In the darkest and loneliest of times, we can't see the way up or out. Understanding what God's presence means...and that of his son is a key. He is always with us. Those times also remind us of his presence and teach us for the next time," she says. Jeremiah 29:11 was inspiration for Alyce: "'For I know the plans I have for you,' declares the Lord, 'plans to prosper you and not to harm you, plans to give you hope and a future.'"

Having "got it" at such a young age, Alyce was able to stay steady during the vicissitudes of her mother's illness. As a consequence, she became a successful attorney, a wife and mother of two children, six grandchildren, and the first woman elected as president of the Alabama State Bar Association.

Conclusion

Peter and Alyce are wonderful role models for us in growing into emotional stability (Peter) and developing emotional stability at an early age even amid chaos (Alyce).

Peter is perhaps the most relatable man in the Bible. He is just so very human. Jesus taught Peter stability as he loved Peter and directed him to step outside of his comfort zone, from all he had known, to become a fisher of men. When Peter became afraid and felt himself sinking under the weight of fear, Jesus was there to say, "Do not be afraid."

When Alyce faced terrifying experiences in her young life, her father, her family, her church, and her heavenly father were there to hold her up, to help her take the tragedy in her life and use it for good as a productive and loving adult.

Both Peter and Alyce show us how we too can build emotional stability in the midst of turmoil by turning to our faith and to those who teach us and hold us up.

Questions For Thought And Reflection

1. How did Jesus help Peter learn to manage his emotions, his volatile temperament? What did Peter find as true stability? Was it the person of Jesus Christ or the truths displayed through Jesus' nature? Both?

2. How did Alyce's family, church, and faith help her maintain emotional stability during the tempestuous times in her young life?

3. How has your temperament evolved throughout your life? How would you describe your temperament now? What has challenged, stretched, and helped you to grow in temperament?

4. Peter's greatest weaknesses, his tempestuousness, his passion, his humanness, may have been his greatest strength. Those same traits may have led to his unique abilities as a leader in spreading Jesus's teachings. Peter's life shows that reining in or re-routing our passion in life gives us the talents we use later in life. How might Peter's life serve as a role model for you?

5. What are some areas that you find difficult to stabilize in your day-to-day life and relationships? Patience? Understanding? Love for the unlovely?

CHAPTER SIX: HABITS

This chapter addresses the emotional intelligence skill of habits: "Habits, as much as memory and reason, are at the root of how we behave. We might not remember the experiences that create our habits, but once they are lodged within our brains, they influence how we act — often without our realization."[95] This chapter focuses on the story of Solomon whose life serves as a lesson in the importance of maintaining healthy emotional habits. We see in the behavioral science section how habits change our brains. Pam's experience of grief after the loss of her husband, Larry, shows how habits impact our lives.

Solomon
Solomon, a son of King David, was appointed to be his successor by his father as David lay ill and dying. Upon his father's death, Solomon prayed for wisdom and the Lord appeared to Solomon:

> "[T]he Lord appeared to Solomon during the night in a dream, and God said, 'Ask for whatever you want me to give you.' Solomon answered, "O Lord my God, you have made your servant king in place of David my father, although I am but a little child. I do not know how to go out or come in…. Give your servant therefore an understanding mind to govern your people, that I may discern between good and evil, for who is able to govern this your great people.
>
> "It pleased the Lord that Solomon had asked this. And God said to him, 'Because you have asked this, and have not asked for yourself long life or riches or the life of your enemies but have asked for yourself understanding to discern what is right, behold, I now do according to your word. Behold, I give you a wise and discerning mind, so that none like you has been before you and none like you shall arise after you. I give you also what you have not asked, both riches and honor, so that no other king shall compare with you, all your days. And if you will walk in my ways, keeping my statutes and my commandments, as your father David walked, then I will lengthen your days.'"[96]

Thereafter, "people came from all the nations to hear from the wisdom of Solomon" (1 Kings 4:34). Solomon became a wise leader who strengthened Israel and, bringing the tribes of Israel together, established "peace on all sides." (1 Kings 4:20).

At some point, however, Solomon began to veer off course. He amassed great wealth, building "a magnificent temple for the Lord, a vast palace for himself and many fine buildings." The Lord came to Solomon, instructing him to "keep all my commandments" (1 Kings 6:11) and warning him: "If you turn aside from following me and do not keep my commandments, but go and serve other gods and worship them, I will cut Israel off from the land...[A]ll you have built will be a "heap of ruins" (1 Kings 9:6).

Solomon did not heed God's warning. Enticed to serve "other gods" by his many wives from other cultures, Solomon's "heart was not true to the Lord his God" (1 Kings 11:4). Consequences followed. Adversaries "who despised Israel" fought Solomon's armies. The years of peace Israel had enjoyed during Solomon's reign ended as Israel was consumed by rebellions and infighting. Israel succumbed to Babylon, and the magnificent temple Solomon had built was destroyed. Israel ceased to exist.

I find the story of Solomon haunting. If Solomon, a person so wise and blessed, could lose his way, what about the rest of us? I think of the sweet, mischievous boy who played little league baseball with my son and had the biggest smile I've ever seen. Joyous, he never met a stranger. In college he partied a lot. One night, he died of a drug overdose after a fraternity party. How did he lose his way? Was it a bad decision that one night or a series of bad decisions that led to his overdose? Does it matter?

I think of a dear colleague who as a young lawyer was passionate about using his law skills to help others. He was, and is, one of the smartest, hardest working, creative lawyers I know. Now, thirty years later, he is rich, feared, sad, lonely, and dissatisfied. Somewhere along the way, he quit focusing on helping others and focused on helping himself. How did he lose his way?

Throughout my life, I have regularly embarked on "big, exciting projects" and become too tired and too stressed to experience the treasures of my life: being present with my husband, my children, my friends. How do I keep losing my way? Across the street lives Barry Mason, one of the wisest, kindest people I've ever met. He has lived a life of grace despite tragedies that would sink the rest of us. Throughout a long, illustrious career, he has mentored hundreds of talented people, watching many of them become happy and successful. He also has seen some lose their way and shatter their lives. I asked Barry what made the difference? Why can some people rein in their worst impulses before it is too late? Why can't all of us?

His answer was short and simple: "They got away from healthy habits." At first I thought Barry meant habits like don't drink or eat too much, get exercise, maintain relationships with family and friends, work at something you care about, don't be greedy, and so on. And he did; but what he was really talking about was habits of faith.

Behavioral Science On Habits

The human brain physically changes when we develop habits. To understand these changes, behavioral scientists study rats by placing wires in their brains and placing the rats in a maze with cheese at the end of the maze. Smelling cheese, the rats dash through the maze as they search for it. The first time a rat runs through the maze, it races down one pathway, hits a dead end, turns around, and races down another, one dead end after another, until finally, it finds the cheese.[97]

Scientists observing the brains of the wired-up rats as they race through the maze watch an "explosion of activity" on the rats' first few efforts to find the cheese. As the rats learn their way through the maze, however, activity in their brains decreases. The rats have formed a habit that leads them to the correct route. The route, the habit, has become automatic.[98]

Studies of humans show the same process. When we engage in behavior that creates a habit, whether it is drinking a cup of coffee as soon as we wake up, or reaching for a shot of vodka, our brains create a pathway for that habit. To create a habit, our brains have to work hard but once a habit is established, it is not hard at all for us to follow that habit because the pathway for it has become automatic. It is hardwired. It takes little or no effort to engage in it. We no longer have to think about how to make our coffee or where to find the shot glass.

Changing a habit is hard, however. We have to resist the automatic pathway we've created in our brains, and we have to put in a lot of energy into creating a new pathway. If we want to cut back on caffeine, we may have to put away the coffee pods and place herbal tea bags in the cabinet where the coffee used to be. If we want to stop drinking vodka we may have to clear out the shot glasses and vodka from our home and go to an early morning AA meeting instead to picking up a shot glass.

In short: creating a new habit is hard, but once we have established a habit, it is easy to follow it, and hard to resist it. It has become hardwired in our brain and is automatic. To change a habit and replace it with a new habit is very hard, for two reasons: first, we have to *resist* the pathway of the old habit, and second, we have to *create* a pathway for the new habit. Both take intentional effort.

Like the rats, like Solomon, we lose our habits if we stop practicing them. If we work all of the time, we get out of the habit of being home for dinner with our family. If we want to rekindle our family dinner habit, we have to resist our established pathway (working late) and re-create a new pathway (working less, leaving before traffic picks up).

Creating a habit, changing a habit, or rekindling a slipped habit requires self-awareness, a desire to change, a plan to change, and specific, behavioral steps. God gave Solomon "nudges" as Solomon slipped into bad habits ("Keep my commandments. If you serve other gods all you have built will be a heap of ruins." 1 Kings 9:6) Solomon either didn't notice the nudges and warnings or chose to ignore them. Do we have nudges? Do we heed these nudges?

Barry Mason says that the key to cultivating good habits is to seek God's help and also do our part. In Barry's words: "God has always provided for all of my needs, even in the midst of unfathomable grief. He was there for me. But I am expected to do my part." Pope Francis agrees with Barry: We are not, the Pope says, to be "passive spectators" but to be "co-creators" with God in our futures.

The Ties That Bind: EQ Habits In Day-To-Day Life

Barry and I had our conversation about habits a number of years ago, early in this book's development. At that time, I had in mind several people to profile for this chapter. I also had what I see now was a fairly limited view of habits. I thought of habits more as ways we enhance our lives. Now I see they can also be what lift us from despair.

Two years ago, my beloved husband, Larry, was diagnosed with early-onset Alzheimer's. He went downhill quickly, from essentially asymptomatic to unable to do any of the activities he loved. He also began experiencing a succession of physical illnesses, including Covid pneumonia in the fall of 2020. He passed away, at home, on October 18, 2020.

Since our first date, my husband and I had been inseparable, whether we were on hundred-mile bike rides, hiking in the woods, playing with grandkids, having dinner with friends, traveling, or sitting side-by-side in the evenings watching a movie. Whatever we were doing, we had fun. Just being together was fun. At work in the middle of the afternoon, I would think, "Oh good, only three more hours and I get to go home and see Larry!"

Given the health issues Larry faced, I guess I should have been prepared to lose him. But I wasn't. I'm not. I still expect him to walk into the house with his joyous smile and our greeting for each other, "Woo Hoo!" Some days I feel like the sadness will eat me alive.

And yet it hasn't. Not yet anyway. New to the community of the grieving, I know I have much to learn, but as I look back on the days after Larry died, I can see that a few habits, habits I did not even realize I was following, are what got me through a day, and then the next day, and the next. I offer what I've learned.

Gratitude, Not Regret
After Larry's death, the kitchen was the most painful place I could be. He and I were always in the kitchen at the same time for breakfast, lunch, and dinner. We were usually at the same counter, right next to the refrigerator, the cutting board, and the sink. We joked about how in our whole house, we were always within the same three feet of space. Standing at that counter alone after he died was unbearable.

During one of those moments, I thought of a time two years before when Larry and I had been in the kitchen together. We were sitting at the kitchen table and had just returned from the neurologist who told us that Larry, age 66, had Alzheimer's. We were shocked. There is no history of Alzheimer's disease in Larry's family. He was in superb health and always had been. I thought of a dear friend whose father had Alzheimer's. He had been bedridden for years in a nursing home. How could Larry have Alzheimer's? We had ridden our bicycles one hundred miles the day before.

The neurologist had been kind and helpful as he talked about the next steps: medications, therapies, our upcoming plans. He advised that we cancel a cycling and hiking trip we had scheduled for the next month in Ireland. "Routine is your friend," he said. "That kind of travel would be difficult." Sadly, we knew what he meant. Our last international trip, a few years before, had been hard. Usually, we found the inevitable travel disruptions to be part of the adventure. On that trip, the disruptions were disorienting for Larry.

As we sat together at the kitchen table, we talked a lot, including about our upcoming trip to Ireland. We had trip cancellation insurance, but to get our money back we had to cancel soon. Talking about canceling that trip made everything very real, very fast. For Larry, planning and taking trips was like having air to breathe. All of his life, he had organized adventures for friends and family — hiking, biking, canoeing, kayaking, camping. Everyone always wanted to go on a Larry Pierson trip. Whether it was camping in the Smoky Mountains, a forty-day cross country bicycle ride, a cycling trip in Italy, or canoeing in rural Alabama, Larry's trips were always fun. Always an adventure.

In tears, I told Larry that I was so, so sorry I had been the reason we had cancelled two recent cycling trips, one on the Camino Way in Spain, and another on the C&O Canal in Maryland and Washington DC with good friends. Both times my work schedule had been overwhelming and I just couldn't face getting ready for the trip or jumping back into a backed-up workload as soon as we got home. Both times Larry was sweet, kind, and understanding, saying, "Don't you worry. We've got the rest of our lives to take trips. We've got plenty of time."

Now, we had run out of time. As I cried, Larry took my hand, looked me in the eye and said, "Don't you worry. Think about all the trips we have taken. I can't imagine anyone taking as many trips as we have." On the day that Larry received what had to be the most devastating news of his life, he was comforting me.

After Larry's death, as I stood at the kitchen counter, alone, in despair, that conversation came back to me. I felt as comforted and soothed as I had when Larry had held my hand and consoled me about our cancelled trips. I realized that what Larry had told me then: focus on the good, not the bad, was how he had lived his life. At that moment, I felt Larry guiding me, just as he had done on hundreds of bike trips.

I willed myself to think about one of my favorite bike rides with Larry. I thought of an overnight trip we took with a dear friend on two beautiful spring days riding along smooth country roads. I remembered funny things Larry said, the breeze as we rode, the clear sky and puffy clouds, the peanut butter and jelly sandwiches we ate for lunch under a tree, the delicious pizza and laughs we shared at dinner. I felt the joy of that trip.

From that moment on, whenever I feel the loneliness and sadness coming over me, I try my best to shift from those feelings to a specific time of joy with Larry. I think about where we were, what the weather was like, who was there, how the sky looked, what the birds sounded like, the jokes we shared, the fun we had.

As a creature who could not find her way through the maze of grief, I am learning my way. Some days, it is really, really hard to shift my thoughts from regret to gratitude. Some days self-pity, fear, obsessing over things I can do nothing about take over, and nothing will beat them back. Sometimes I feel foolish, trying something so hokey in the face of my unfathomable grief. Sometimes I am so worn down from sadness, I can't summon the strength to shift my thoughts. Some days, it is easy to ignore the nudge. But I'm finding that the more I try to do my part, to shift my thoughts, to remember the advice Larry gave me, the more I feel God beside me helping me along.

Helping Others
My brain did not work well in the weeks after Larry died, but I knew a few things. I knew I was saddest when I was alone, especially in our house. But it was complicated to get together with other people, even family who could help comfort and distract me. Sometimes, usually when I least expected it, being around others, hearing them reminisce about Larry or just seeing them happy, made me sadder. Also, Covid was rampant, there were no treatments or vaccines, the world was in lockdown, winter weather made outdoor gatherings impossible. Everyone I knew was isolating. I was alone a lot.

In desperate loneliness, I called Diane Lewis, the director of Tuscaloosa's Meals on Wheels. Until shortly before Larry's death, he and I had delivered meals twice a week. I asked Diane if she still needed volunteers to deliver the meals. She did.

I didn't return to delivering Meals on Wheels because the program badly needed more volunteers. I didn't return to help the clients. Those thoughts never occurred to me; however true they were. I returned to get out of my sad, empty house and because Meals on Wheels suited my needs perfectly. There would be interaction with other people but on a limited basis, so there would not be much of a chance I would have a meltdown. Delivering the meals was covid-safe. All volunteers and clients wore masks, no one is indoors, and everyone socially distances whether picking up or delivering meals.

Returning to Meals on Wheels was a tonic for me. It was wonderful to see Diane and the Meals on Wheels staff, to visit with the other volunteers as we waited for the meals to arrive, and especially, to see the clients. Every Meals on Wheels client I've ever met greets you with joy and gratitude. They are effusive in their appreciation. Accepting their deep-felt thank you's for a plastic-wrapped styrofoam box will jolt anyone out of self- absorption. When I was delivering meals, I quit thinking about myself. I couldn't focus on being sad as I looked up directions, found my way to the correct house, and greeted clients.

Delivering the meals reset my perspective. It was impossible not to feel grateful about what I had in my life when I was delivering meals to the clients. Most of them deal daily with difficulties the rest of us cannot fathom. Some are in terrible health and can barely manage to get to their door. Many live in poverty and in dangerous neighborhoods. Most have outlived loved ones and are alone. When clients open their doors to cold, dark interiors, you know that the meal you deliver will be the only food they will eat that day and that you are the only person they will see. Handing meals to the clients reminded me that even in the midst of my grief, I was incredibly lucky. I could still walk, drive, and go home to a comfortable house with food in the refrigerator. I may have been taking food to clients, but they were nourishing me. Their strength lifted me up. Their gratitude was balm for my soul.

Considering that a completely impure, selfish motive led me to something that helped me so profoundly, I have to smile. Isn't it amazing how sometimes we are led to just what we need when we don't have the sense to know it? When do we do the right thing for all of the wrong reasons? God works in funny ways sometimes.

Growing In Faith

For years, I taught middle school and high school Sunday School classes. I loved it. I loved the kids' energy and questions, the other teachers I taught with, and hanging out on the youth floor. One year, a few weeks before Easter, I realized I was scheduled to teach the Easter lesson on Jesus' resurrection. That was a problem.

I am about as right-brained, concrete, literal, logical, and evidence-based as a person could possibly be (no surprise I'm a lawyer). I often don't get jokes. Sarcasm goes right past me. Faith questions pose a big dilemma. I cannot figure out what it means that Jesus is fully human and fully divine or how the virgin birth, atonement, or especially, resurrection works.

For good reason, I was concerned how I would present the resurrection lesson. I didn't feel comfortable sharing my questions with impressionable teenagers. But I knew some of the kids would ask the things I've always wondered about: How does someone who is dead come back alive, fold up their clothes, and open a tomb? How does a dead person speak? Does their voice sound the same as it did when they were alive? What did Jesus look like after his resurrection? How come no one recognized him but knew it was Jesus? Did Thomas really feel Jesus's wounds? I knew my efforts to skirt the kids' questions would be like sugar to bees. All fifty-plus of them would swarm with the tough questions.

About a week or so before Easter, I was driving by the homeless shelter for men in downtown Birmingham. The shelter opens at 5 PM and stays open until it reaches capacity. Each day, it is first come, first serve as to who will be able to stay the night, eat a hot meal, get a shower, and sleep in a safe place. It was about 4:30 PM when I drove by the shelter. There were forty or fifty men outside the shelter, waiting for it to open. Most were sitting on the sidewalk leaning against the building. A few were asleep or passed out on the concrete. Several were noticeably drunk, high, or otherwise agitated. Some were talking or yelling to themselves. All of the men were disheveled with unkempt hair and ragged clothes. They had dirty, tired faces. They looked like they had given up. As I sat in my car, waiting for the light to change, I wondered how any of them could possibly rebuild their lives.

As I sat waiting for the light, one of the men leaning against the shelter made eye contact with me. He waved. I waved back. He smiled. I smiled back. The light changed, and I drove on. Just past the shelter I saw a tree stump in a dirt square in the sidewalk. There were trees growing in other squares. Those trees had green leafy branches. The stump, which appeared to have burned, was short, black, and charred. But it had one, tiny shoot of green leaves.

I thought back to the men, so worn and beat down. I thought of the man who smiled and waved at me. I realized that just like the stump that appeared to be dead but was growing new life, those men held within them the possibility of new life. They were not beyond hope. Maybe, I thought, whatever happened two thousand years ago in a tomb in Jerusalem, Jesus's resurrection means that none of us, however dead we may seem, are beyond the hope of new life. I realized I had my resurrection Sunday school lesson.

I don't know if any of the wiggly teenagers in my Sunday school class that Easter learned a thing about resurrection, but I sure did. I learned that although I can't figure out whether or how Jesus returned from the dead long ago, that's okay, because God is more mysterious than I can comprehend. What I do know is that I've seen resurrection a lot.

I've seen the dead come alive from addiction, exhaustion, violence, anger, and brokenness. I've seen how resurrection is not limited to literal rebirth of the physical body or limited to Jesus. I have felt my deceased loved ones with me. I've heard my dad's advice, "Be kind, patient, wise," just when I need it. As I rush around and spill, drop, break, or forget things in my haste, I see my grandfather showing a five-year old me how erasing words slowly works a lot better than ramming the eraser across the paper. Every time I'm in my yard, I feel my grandmother's joy as she tended her snapdragons. Many days I feel Larry right beside me. I hear the advice he would give me and how he would say it. When I feel overwhelmed, I feel him saying, "Don't you worry. We've got this."

Since Larry died, my faith has continued to grow because now, I know that resurrection is, for all of us.

Where Do Habits Come From?

In the days after Larry died, it never occurred to me that focusing on gratitude, helping others, or growing in my faith were habits that would pull me out of the darkness of grief.

As I think back now, I can see that each of these habits has been a gift from others and that they were given to me a long time ago. Twenty years ago, during a sad and scary time in my life, a friend suggested that I keep a gratitude journal. I had never heard of such, but she convinced me to give it a try. From that friend, I learned the power of gratitude.

When I was growing up, my father took my sister and me, in the Christmas dresses our Mom had made, to see the "shut-ins" in our church. The shut-ins were widowed, elderly, and homebound. Their houses were hot, the treats they gave us were yummy, and they were happy to see us. I will always remember how good it felt to see them so happy. From my parents, I learned the magic of helping others.

As a kid, I asked a lot of questions. I'm sure they irritated the fool out of whomever I was interrogating. But parents, my Sunday School teachers, and my youth leaders always welcomed my questions about God. From them, I learned that wrestling with my doubts was a good thing, that it is the way we grow in our faith and keep it alive and real in every stage of life.

As I think back to the gifts of good habits I have been given, I also think about the habits I've learned all by myself, some very destructive. They too have been with me a long time. Their pathways are well-worn in my brain. These habits can easily grab hold of me and take me down a dark path. When they do, I try to think about Solomon and how he let his bad habits take over his good habits. I try to pay attention to the "God nudges" that tell me to focus on gratitude, not regret, to help others, and always, to grow in my faith.

Conclusion
Habits can serve us well or bring us down. Like Solomon, we all lose our way if we slide into unhealthy habits. Habits like gratitude, helping others, and growing in our faith can bring us joy, and when we need it, lift us from despair. It is fitting to close this chapter with the words of Barry Mason, Pam's wise friend, who shared the habits of faith he aspires to follow:

> *"Reducing things in my life that may be important but not essential, being more conscious in how I use my time because once gone it can never be recovered, focusing more on the needs of others, avoid potentially stressful situations, continuing to identify things that make me feel relevant and purposeful, limiting my social contacts to persons whose life and actions I admire, more time building heightened awareness of unchanging eternal truths, being more aware of the wonders in simple everyday things like a beautiful flower or listening to a bird singing."*

Questions For Thought And Reflection

1. We've all had journeys into despair. That is part of life. Think about a difficult time you've had, whether it was the death of a loved one, illness, disappointment, divorce, addiction. Did certain habits help you? Could they have? Could they still?

2. Have you experienced "God nudges"? What did they feel like? How did you know? Was it something someone said? Something in the situation? Did you make changes based on the nudge? Are you getting nudges in your life now? What changes might you make?

3. Some habits serve us well in one stage of life but not in others. Is it time in your life to leave behind certain habits or tweak them?

4. Do you have habits of faith? What are they? Do they serve you well? If not, what changes would you like to make?

CHAPTER SEVEN: SELF-REGULATION

Either we control our emotions, or they control us. This chapter examines this truth. The ability to regulate our emotions is described as the "master skill of emotional intelligence."[99] It requires that we recognize the emotions we are feeling, understand the causes of our emotions, and appreciate how our emotions influence our thoughts and decisions. In this chapter, we look at the life of King David, the behavioral science on regulating emotions, and the story of Tammy, a Ph.D. student currently in federal custody. As we will see, both King David and Tammy provide lessons on practical strategies for controlling emotions.

David

The Bible tells the story of David's reign in detail reflecting its importance as well as its length (1 Samuel 16 to 1 Kings 2). David "reigned over Israel for forty years, seven and a half in Hebron and 33 in Jerusalem."[100] His long reign was later regarded as Israel's "golden age"; David himself was seen as the model king.[101] But before he became King, we may remember David as the small boy who slayed the giant, Goliath:

> "David said to Saul, 'Let no one lose heart on account of this Philistine [Goliath]; your servant will go and fight him.' Saul replied, 'You are not able to go out against this Philistine and fight him; you are only a young man, and he has been a warrior from his youth.' 'The Lord who rescued me from the paw of the lion and the paw of the bear will rescue me from the hand of this Philistine.' Saul said to David, 'Go, and the Lord be with you.'
>
> Then Saul dressed David in his own tunic. He put a coat of armor on him and a bronze helmet on his head. David fastened on his sword over the tunic and tried walking around, because he was not used to them. "I cannot go in these," he said to Saul, "because I am not used to them." So, he took them off. Then he took his staff in his hand, chose five smooth stones from the stream, put them in the pouch of his shepherd's bag and, with his sling in his hand, approached the Philistine.

> "Meanwhile, the Philistine, with his shield bearer in front of him, kept coming closer to David. He looked David over and saw that he was little more than a boy, glowing with health and handsome, and he despised him.
>
> "David said to the Philistine, 'You come against me with sword and spear and javelin, but I come against you in the name of the Lord Almighty, the God of the armies of Israel, whom you have defied. This day the Lord will deliver you into my hands, and I'll strike you down and cut off your head. This very day I will give the carcasses of the Philistine army to the birds and the wild animals, and the whole world will know that there is a God in Israel. All those gathered here will know that it is not by sword or spear that the Lord saves; for the battle is the Lord's, and he will give all of you into our hands.'"
>
> "As the Philistine moved closer to attack him, David ran quickly toward the battle line to meet him. Reaching into his bag and taking out a stone, he slung it and struck the Philistine on the forehead. The stone sank into his forehead, and he fell face down on the ground. So David triumphed over the Philistine with a sling and a stone; without a sword in his hand he struck down the Philistine and killed him." (*Various verses from I Samuel 17*).

The voice inside David to fight Goliath was the intelligent emotional voice that came from God. David was able to self-regulate and calm his own fears, disbelief, doubt, and he defeated a giant.

After David became king, he remained capable of regulating his emotions. For example, although given the clear opportunity to kill King Saul who was hunting him down to kill him, David exercised restraint and did not kill God's anointed:

> "Saul took three thousand able young men from all Israel and set out to look for David and his men near the crags of the wild goats. He came to the sheep pens along the way; a cave was there, and Saul went in to relieve himself.
>
> "David and his men were far back in the cave. The men said, "This is the day the Lord spoke of when he said to you, 'I will give your enemy into your hands for you to deal with as you wish.'" Then David crept up unnoticed and cut off a corner of Saul's robe." (1 Samuel 24:2-4)

David took the corner of Saul's robe to prove to Saul afterwards that he was obedient to God's commands not to harm God's anointed and that he intended Saul no harm. His faithfulness to God over the years made him a "man after God's own heart," and he achieved Israel's kingship. He regulated his desires and brought intelligence to his emotions as he led first his armies then his kingdom. But his failure to self-regulate in one instance, to employ that emotional intelligence tool in the case of Bathsheba, had catastrophic consequences.

David, like all human beings, was a complex character with emotions ranging over a broad spectrum. He was a wise leader as king, but he also succumbed to temptation when he committed adultery and later, murder, to have whom and what he wanted... Bathsheba.

> *"One evening David got up from his bed and walked around on the roof of the palace. From the roof he saw a woman bathing. The woman was very beautiful, and David sent someone to find out about her.*
>
> *"The man said, 'She is Bathsheba, the daughter of Eliam and the wife of Uriah the Hittite.' Then David sent messengers to get her. She came to him, and he slept with her. (Now she was purifying herself from her monthly uncleanness.) Then she went back home. The woman conceived and sent word to David, saying, 'I am pregnant.*
>
> *"In the morning David wrote a letter to Joab.... In it he wrote, "Put Uriah out in front where the fighting is fiercest. Then withdraw from him so he will be struck down and die."*
>
> *"So, while Joab had the city under siege, he put Uriah at a place where he knew the strongest defenders were. When the men of the city came out and fought against Joab, some of the men in David's army fell; moreover, Uriah the Hittite died.*
>
> *"When Uriah's wife heard that her husband was dead, she mourned for him. After the time of mourning was over, David had her brought to his house, and she became his wife and bore him a son. But the thing David had done displeased the Lord."* (2 Samuel 11:2-5, 14-17, 26-27)

The life of David demonstrates the crucial importance, difficulty, and conflict of self-regulation and how this emotional intelligence skill requires lifelong effort. The voice inside David to fight Goliath, to not kill Saul, to deal compassionately with his son, Absalom, are all examples of the intelligent emotional voice within David. David's failure to regulate his emotions when he allowed lust to overcome morality, a choice which had catastrophic consequences for another human being, also came from within David.

No one ever said that being able to manage our emotions is easy or that we don't all make mistakes. We do, and we will. But let us note that David's failure was one that God would use in David's life as God can use our failures in life. Thankfully, we serve a God of second, third, and fourth chances, for he is a God of love as shown by the fact that David remained "a man after God's own heart."

Behavioral Science Of Self-Regulation

To have emotional intelligence, we must manage our emotional life with the intelligence we have been given by the God who created us. "Our passions, when well-exercised, have wisdom; they guide our thinking, our values, our survival. But they can easily go awry, and all too often they do. The problem is not with emotionality, but with the appropriateness of emotion and its expression. The question is, how can we bring intelligence to our emotions?"[102]

According to M. M. Kobiruzzaman, "Self-reflection is the capacity to control feelings and pressures. People who possess self-regulation …think before acting and don't make careless decisions. They are able to say no and change themselves if situations demand it."[103] Learning to regulate our emotions requires self-awareness. It requires that we be aware enough to recognize the emotions we are experiencing (anger, fear, anxiety, and so on), to understand the causes of our emotions, and to appreciate how our emotions influence our thoughts and decisions. As Daniel Goleman summarizes:

> "Understanding emotions involves 'reading' a situation, asking first, what is happening, including events that led up to it, and second, how our emotions have shifted as a result. This will help us determine our goals in the situation and identify what regulation strategies we should use to meet them."[104]

To take one example: recognizing that we are experiencing the emotion of anger and that the cause of our anger is not what Joe, or Jan, or whoever, has just said to us but that we may be reliving another, hurtful time in our life that has nothing to do with the current situation, is an excellent first step in emotional regulation. Learning strategies to control our behavior until we can regulate our emotions is another step of self-regulation. Instead of punching a hole in the wall to rid ourselves of our anger, we can seek to develop habits for times of emotional turmoil such as taking a deep breath or excusing ourselves from the situation. Instead of summoning Bathsheba, for example, David could have one of his wives, or diverted his attention by engaging in duties or music.

Below, we meet Tammy and see the emotional intelligence she has used and is using to overcome emotions of fear, anger, inadequacy, and the destructive conduct in which she had been engaging. Let her courage, honesty, and fortitude be a model for all of us.

Tammy

Tammy was born into a life of poverty on September 10, 1969, to a thirteen-year-old mother and a seventeen-year-old father in Wilcox County, Alabama. Her father joined the Air Force soon after she was born; her brother was born three years later. Tammy's family moved a lot during her early childhood. But everywhere they moved, "there was chaos at home." Her parents "fought like the teenagers they were, then would disappear to their bedroom to make up." Tammy and her brother dealt with the chaos in different ways: he acted out while Tammy internalized responsibility for the problems.

When Tammy was seven years old, her parents divorced, and Tammy and her brother went to live with their maternal grandmother in Clarke County, Alabama. Their grandmother was a deeply religious woman, and they went to church "every time the doors were open." At some point, Tammy "grasped the idea that if I acted good enough, God would fix all my problems." This idea was solidified by what she heard every time the pastor preached: you are a sinner; you are going to hell unless you become more like Jesus. Tammy was terrified that if she were not good enough, she too would "die by being nailed to a cross and then burn in hell forever." She recounts how she "cannot recall ever hearing that God loved me except in the Sunday School song I learned—*Jesus loves me this I know, for the Bible tells me so, little ones to him belong, they are weak, but he is strong*, But I could not see where God loved me."

The chaos in Tammy's family continued. Her dad would not pay child support, had very little to do with Tammy's brother and her, and began another family. Her mother moved to another city. Her grandmother worked a lot. As Tammy remembers, "In my mind, I was responsible for all these problems. I became exhausted trying to act good enough so God would fix my family. I decided I might as well find ways to be happy here on earth since the afterlife was going to be so bad."

As a teenager, Tammy discovered boys and marijuana. Her mother took her to her first bar at age fourteen. She felt at home: "As soon as I walked into that bar, I knew I had arrived where I belonged—the smoky air, the band playing loud, the people on the dance floor. I fell in love with alcohol and the whole partying lifestyle that night."

Over the next thirty years, Tammy went through five marriages and five divorces. She became addicted to crack cocaine, going through several periods of recovery and relapse. Somehow during the thirty years of marriages, divorces, addiction, recovery, and relapse, Tammy obtained her bachelor's and master's degree in social work and completed one year of a PhD program "before my addiction became more important than my education." At that point, she "gave up on her life's dream of becoming a researcher, writer, and educator. I was tired of trying."

In 2018, Tammy was charged in federal court with seven felonies and two misdemeanors. When arrested, Tammy realized that "the only option left for me was to face my addiction and recover." She began to "intentionally examine how I treated other people, pausing before I made smart remarks, thinking about how to be kind, and started treating people how I wanted to be treated."

On December 27, 2018, at an AA meeting Tammy attended while in rehab, "the chairperson read the following from the "We Agnostics" chapter of the book *Alcoholics Anonymous*:

> "When we became alcoholics, crushed by a self-imposed crisis we could not postpone or evade, we had to fearlessly face the proposition that either God is everything or else he is nothing. God either is, or he isn't. What was our choice to be?" [105]

As Tammy described:

> "I had a visceral reaction. At that moment, I felt a heavy weight lift out of my body. All the tension left my shoulders and a peace like I have never felt entered my body. I released my self-reliance and accepted that there is a God that loves

and cares for me. No matter how badly I have messed up my life, he has always been there protecting me, waiting for that moment, in that meeting, for me to allow him in my life."

The next morning, Tammy went outside, looked up to the sky and shouted: "What do you want me to do?" She heard: "Do my work." Tammy began work on herself. She learned "to tell the truth about myself, to trust other people, to have faith in the recovery process and God, to hold tight to hope for a better future, and to love all the people in my life."

In March 2020, Tammy applied to and was accepted into the Higher Education Administration doctoral program at The University of Alabama. She began work on her doctorate. Six months later, she signed a binding five-year plea agreement on the federal charges and entered federal custody. Released in 2024, Tammy is rebuilding her life and helping others rebuild theirs.

The Ties That Bind: Self-Regulation In Day-To-Day Life
The lives of King David and Tammy show how self-regulation of emotions requires a lifelong effort. As a young man, David was able to regulate his emotions. He was able to calm his fears, disbelief, and doubt, and defeat the giant, Goliath. But David failed to regulate his emotions of desire and greed when he was tempted by lust for Bathsheba and ordered the murder of Uriah.

Tammy was able to regulate her emotions of desire and craving for alcohol the many times she went to rehab and recovery and set her life on a productive path of education and betterment. But she was unable to fully overcome her addictive urges until she was able to feel God's strength within her.

Thankfully, God never gives up on us. Thankfully, we serve a God of second, third, fourth, endless chances, because God is not the unforgiving, hard God Tammy heard about in church as a child. He is a God of love. God gave David another chance. When confronted by Nathan about his wrongful behavior regarding Bathsheba and Uriah, David realized he had sinned and repented ("I have sinned against the Lord." 2 Samuel 12:13). David learned how to get himself back on track, and how, once again, to listen to God's voice.

In treatment, Tammy realized that God was there for her, even in the midst of her addiction. Like David who went on to live life with purpose and meaning, Tammy has found purpose in her life: "I will treat my incarceration as an opportunity to collect data for my dissertation and to help other women in federal prison find peace through recovery. Not only will I finish my doctoral degree upon release from prison, but I will open a residential recovery facility. I have resisted the purpose God has for my life far too long, but through this difficult process that I am in now, I surrender."

The ability to recognize and regulate our emotions and develop productive skills for dealing with the upsetting emotions all of us experience enables us to move beyond negative behavior and engage in productive acts. Emotional intelligence is recognizing this choice and choosing to walk the path that reflects God's image. The God-image imprinted in each of us can give us the emotional intelligence we need to slay our Goliaths.

Conclusion

Self-regulation is a choice for each of us. The tool of self-regulation works to dispel our false thoughts and enables us to move into positive action. This tool also protects us from negative actions. We can choose to run into battle with our Goliaths or hide in the background and hope the giants will be defeated.

Both David and Tammy fought to surrender their emotions to God's plan for their lives and to acquire and employ the emotional intelligence skill of self-regulation. May their lives be an example to all of us that it can be done, that the battle to surrender never ends, and that God never gives up on us.

Questions And Thoughts For Reflection

1. Self-regulation is a skill that can be learned, grown, and enhanced. How have you seen your ability to regulate your emotions grow throughout your life?

2. David, as a boy, faced a giant without fear, knowing God's armor and protection was with him. How have you handled your "Goliath battles"? How would you handle them now with the benefit of life experience, hindsight?

3. In ancient times, "a knight's plate armor would be cleaned by hand with a mixture of sand or brick dust, and vinegar or urine

to make an abrasive paste.[106] Behavioral scientists identify strategies to help regulate our emotions: delay, deflect, reframe, breathe deep slow breaths, and more. These strategies can be our armor for the times when our emotions threaten to overwhelm our judgment. How have you, might you, use these as your armor? What are the times of emotional turmoil you can anticipate so that you have your armor handy?

4. One of the strategies for regulating emotions is to have a game plan, a set of habits, for difficult situations we can anticipate. For example, if you anticipate that you will be interacting with a negative person, what's your game plan to stay calm, not get upset, not lash out or say things you regret, not absorb their negativity?

> In this regard, it is interesting to look at how David handled a difficult encounter with Eliab, one of his brothers. Do you think David may have been able to fall back on a "game plan" that had worked well for him previously in interactions with his older brothers?
>> *"David asked the men who were standing with him, 'What will be done for the man who kills this Philistine and removes this disgrace from Israel? The people told him about the offer [to slay Goliath], saying, 'That is what will be done for the man who kills him.'*
>> *"Now Eliab [David's] oldest brother heard [David ask this question]. Eliab's anger was aroused against David, and he said, 'Why did you come down here? And with whom have you left those few sheep in the wilderness? I know your pride and the insolence of your heart, for you have come down to see the bloody battle!'*
>> *"'What is it with you?' replied David to Eliab. 'All I did was ask a question.' Ignoring his brother, David turned to someone else, and continued [his conversation about the offer to the man who killed Goliath]"* (1 Samuel 17:27-30).

Note how David stayed calm when his brother chastised him, seeking to embarrass him. David answered Eliab and remained unruffled and confident despite his brother's demeaning tone and words.

CHAPTER EIGHT: SELF-AWARENESS

This chapter focuses on self-awareness, the "keystone of emotional intelligence."[107] We look at the Old Testament story of Moses and how he grew into self-awareness. We move next to behavioral science on self-awareness, in particular the stages of self-awareness which Moses demonstrated for us. We introduce a contemporary mental health hero, Betty Shirley, who like Moses, grew into extraordinary self-awareness. We conclude by applying what we have seen in this chapter to day-to-day life.

Moses

When he was a young man, Moses, in fury, beat a man to death. Clearly, he was not able to regulate his emotions well.

> *"In the course of time Moses grew up. Then he went to see his own people and watched them suffering under forced labor. He saw a Hebrew, one of his own people, being beaten by an Egyptian. He looked all around, and when he didn't see anyone, he beat the Egyptian to death and hid the body in the sand.*
>
> *"When Moses went there the next day, he saw two Hebrew men fighting. He asked the one who started the fight. 'Why are you beating another Hebrew?'*
>
> *"The man asked, 'Who made you our ruler and judge? Are you going to kill me as you killed the Egyptian?'" Then Moses was afraid and thought that everyone knew what he had done.*
>
> *"When Pharaoh heard what Moses had done, he tried to have him killed. But Moses fled from Pharaoh and settled in the land of Midian" (Exodus 2:11-15.)*

In Midian, where Moses fled after committing the murder, Moses married and became a shepherd. He had been in Midian many years when one day, while he was tending the sheep, he saw a burning bush:

> *"Now Moses was tending the flock of Jethro his father-in-law, the priest of Midian, and he led the flock to the far side of the wilderness and came to Horeb, the mountain of God. There the angel of the Lord appeared to him in flames of fire from within a bush. Moses saw that though the bush was on fire it did not burn up. Moses thought, 'I will go over and see this strange*

> sight—why the bush does not burn up.' When the Lord saw that he had gone over to look, God called to him from within the bush, 'Moses! Moses!'
>
> "And Moses said, 'Here I am.'
>
> "'Do not come any closer,' God said. 'Take off your sandals, for the place where you are standing is holy ground.' Then he said, 'I am the God of your father, the God of Abraham, the God of Isaac and the God of Jacob.' At this, Moses hid his face, because he was afraid to look at God" (Exodus 3:1-6).

God told Moses that he was to lead the people of Israel out of their bondage in Egypt. Moses's response was disbelief. God met Moses in his disbelief and assured him:

> "Then the Lord said, I have surely seen the affliction of my people who are in Egypt and have heard their cry because of their taskmasters. I know their sufferings, and I have come down to deliver them out of the hand of the Egyptians and to bring them up out of that land to a good and broad land, a land flowing with milk and honey, to the place of the Canaanites, the Hittites, the Amorites, the Perizzites, the Hivites, and the Jebusites. And now, behold, the cry of the people of Israel has come to me, and I have also seen the oppression with which the Egyptians oppress them. Come, I will send you to Pharaoh that you may bring my people, the children of Israel, out of Egypt" (Exodus 7-10.)

When Moses protested, "Who am I that I should go to Pharaoh and bring the Israelites out of Egypt?" God assured Moses, "I will be with you." Each time Moses raised a concern about his ability to lead the Israelites from Egypt, God gently reminded Moses that he, God, would be with him. God would offer words and proof for people to see.

Note Moses' exceptional self-awareness: of the voice telling him what to do, of the concerns he had in following the direction given to him, in hearing the reassurance of that voice. This story demonstrates two things. One is that Moses, like all of us, was created in the image of God and for that reason, we are capable of more than we ever dreamed. And the second is that many of us miss the burning bush telling us what we need to know because we are not self-aware.

As a young man, Moses only had his emotions. As he grew in the Lord, he acquired an awareness of his emotions, an awareness not just of his feelings but also of his thoughts about his feelings. After forty years in the desert, Moses had plenty of time to know himself, to acquire the self-awareness that he lacked as a young man in Egypt. He was still passionate about the cause of his people, but he had had time to reflect on his weaknesses, especially the destructiveness of his impulsiveness. He had become "aware of both his mood and his thoughts about his mood."[108] He had had time to learn to be aware of his feelings and to act to change them.

Instead of impulsively striking out as he had years before in murdering the Egyptian official or running away in fear at the voice of God, Moses remained calm and rationally explained to God in the burning bush his shortcomings in a negotiation over leadership of the Hebrews. His ability to hear God's voice inside him helped Moses identify and manage his emotions.

Moses' calm, rational, response (Exodus 3:3) is epitomized in his reaction to the snake. He was fearful of the snake (Exodus 4:3), but his faith cast out his fearful feelings so that he could even pick it up at God's command (Exodus 4:4). Moses was able to articulate rationally his limitations (Exodus 3:11 and 4:10) and the formidable obstacles (Exodus 4:1) he foresaw. Voicing his concerns gave God, Moses' inner voice, the opportunity to address Moses's concerns. After "discussing" with God, Moses said, "Yes." He listened to his gut feeling (the Holy Spirit) and became fully aware of himself. He realized that God was in him, and he was in God.

His self-awareness at this point in his life empowered Moses to choose from an array of options to say "Yes" and to approach the burning bush. He could have hidden or denied what he saw.

Or he could have become engulfed with fear and fled. Instead, Moses had learned to be aware of his feelings and used that power to make good decisions in the most critical encounter of his life.[109]

Note the courage and honesty Moses displayed in his self-awareness. He was able to see and ask the hard questions he felt: Who am I? What if they ask me something I don't know? What if people don't believe me? I don't speak eloquently; would you just send someone else?! What wonderful modeling of self-awareness, for if we aren't honest about our feelings, how can we deal with them? How can we seek help from God for them?

To look at how Moses grew into what became extraordinary, otherworldly self-awareness, let us turn to behavioral science.

Behavioral Science On Self-Awareness

Daniel Goleman, one of the foremost experts in the science of emotional intelligence defines self-awareness as:

> "Self-awareness, in short, means being aware of both our mood and our thoughts about that mood.... An inability to notice our true feelings leaves us at their mercy."[110]

Goleman describes self-awareness as a "neutral mode"[111] that maintains self-reflection even amidst turbulent emotions. It is a layer of attention over the feelings that otherwise would get carried away, leading us to overreact and amplify what we perceive. As Goleman notes, "people who have some sophistication about their emotional lives are autonomous and sure of their own boundaries, are in good psychological health, and tend to have a positive outlook on life. When they get into a bad mood they don't ruminate and obsess about it and are able to get out of it sooner. In short, their mindfulness helps them manage their emotions."[112]

Goleman gives the following example of how self-awareness can have a powerful effect on strong, aversive feelings, helping us to avoid poor decisions:

> "A belligerent samurai, an old Japanese tale goes, once challenged a Zen master to explain the concept of heaven and hell. But the monk replied with scorn, 'You're nothing but a lout — I can't waste my time with the likes of you.'
>
> "His very honor attacked, the samurai flew into a rage and, pulling his sword from its scabbard, yelled 'I could kill you for your impertinence.'
>
> "'That,' the monk calmly replied, 'is hell.'
>
> "Startled at seeing the truth in what the master pointed out about the fury that had him in its grip, the samurai calmed down, sheathed his sword, and bowed, thanking the monk for the insight.
>
> "'And that,' said the monk, 'is heaven.'"[113]

Awareness of our feelings can prevent ruinous decisions. As Goleman explains, "The sudden awakening of the samurai to his own agitated state illustrates the crucial difference between being caught up in a feeling and becoming aware that you are being swept away by it."[114] In this way, self-awareness of our strong feelings, whether rage, fear, or sadness, and the havoc they can create in our decision-making, can prevent ruinous decisions.

Behavioral scientists identify three components of self-awareness[115]:

- *Emotional awareness.* "Recognizing a feeling *as it happens* is the keystone of emotional intelligence."[116] When we are unable to recognize our feelings, "we are left at the mercy" of our true feelings. "People with greater certainty about their feelings are better pilots of their lives, having a surer sense of how they really feel about personal decisions from whom to marry to what job to take."[117]

- *Recognizing the effects of our emotions.* If I am in a bad mood, I can deal with it better if I know why I'm in a bad mood. Is it because I am fearful about an upcoming event, angry from a recent encounter, ashamed of something I've done? Some days, it takes courage, and a willingness to forgive (another or ourselves) to honestly grapple with the effects of our emotions. Perceiving the effects of our emotions "can have a powerful impact on how we react," the next step of self-awareness.[118]

- *Taking constructive steps to keep emotions from controlling us.* Once we are aware of what emotions we are truly feeling, we can take constructive steps to deal with them. If I recognize that the reason I'm in a bad mood is because I am fearful about an upcoming event, for example, I can practice harder, ask someone to go with me, or obtain more information about the event. Just planning these steps, much less doing them, will help alleviate my fear or much of it. On the other hand, if I am angry about a recent encounter with a friend, I can work to calm myself down by thinking about things from that person's point of view or past kindnesses by that person. If I am ashamed about something I've done, I can right the wrong I've done by extending an apology, writing in a journal, or going outside for a walk.[119] As Daniel Goleman says, "Emotional self-awareness is the building block of being able to shake off a bad mood."[120]

We have seen how Moses grew into extraordinary self-awareness. Let us now turn to a modern-day hero, who like Moses, grew into self-awareness — of her own illness, what was needed to become well, and what God had in mind for her life.

Betty Shirley: Hero For Mental Health

Betty Shirley was born in Montgomery, Alabama, in the early twentieth century. She married George Shirley of Tuscaloosa who would become the President and CEO of the First National Bank of Tuscaloosa. Together they had three strong daughters who like their parents continue to make huge contributions to the quality of life in Alabama.

As a young adult, Betty showed signs of major anxiety and depression. In her thirties, Betty's signs of depression grew increasingly disturbing. As her illness worsened, George took her everywhere he could find for help. Betty's first shock treatments helped, but ultimately, she needed more help. George tried to avoid committing her to the state mental health institution which, at that time, was in a terrible state of disrepair and on the verge of being taken over by the federal courts for inadequacy.[121] His love for his wife, however, overcame those obstacles, and Betty entered Bryce Hospital upon the recommendation of the psychiatrists who were treating her. At Bryce, Betty was prescribed the right combination of medications, and her condition improved dramatically.

In the course of her treatment at Bryce Hospital, Betty acquired sufficient self-awareness to learn to manage the illness of depression. She attributes her emergence from the depths of depression not only to the greatness of her doctors and the care she received at Bryce but even more, to her faith in God and the power of prayer that she deepened in the course of her treatment. Her awareness that she was a beloved child of God and her love for her family fueled her determination to overcome her illness.

And it provided even more fuel: fuel to change her world. Because of Betty's public commitment to the cause of mental health treatment, seeking therapy in her community holds far less stigma than in many other communities. She has worked tirelessly to promote mental health, from raising enormous funding for mental health facilities to serving as a conduit for individuals in mental health crisis to find the professional help they need in a timely fashion. The latter is no small feat, given the paucity of mental health professionals in Alabama. And the former has been so significant that the mental health clinic at the University of Alabama Medical Center has been named the Betty Shirley Clinic in her honor.

Betty repeatedly acknowledges the awareness she has acquired over the course of her life: that she is "blessed." She was blessed as a child by a family who passed along their faith in God to her, as an adult by a husband who refused to give up until they found the help she needed to treat her mental health disease, and blessed to realize that she is a beloved child of God. Betty's self- awareness is the power that has fueled her ability to manage her depression and to make an enormous difference in the lives of countless other children of God.

The Ties That Bind: Self-Awareness In Day-To-Day Life

Both Moses and Betty heard the still, quiet voice, the gut feeling Goleman references. Moses turned to see the burning bush. He was able to hear God's message when who knows how many others had not. Moses turned to God with his questions, concerns, and worries. When Betty was hospitalized, she too prayed, raised her concerns, and listened. She heard God's call to her, to seek help for her illness. When she received care, she heard God's call again, that she serve others by bravely acknowledging her own journey to mental health and thereby empowering others to seek help. Betty's journey has brought health to an entire community that has extraordinary mental health services because of Betty's brave advocacy. In another recognition of her formidable contributions, President George Bush named her a "Point of Life."

As noted, behavioral scientists have identified three steps in true self-awareness, each of which are demonstrated by Moses and Betty. Both *recognized their emotions and the effect of their emotions*. Moses recognized his feelings of fear and inadequacy and how they were hindering him in leading the Jewish people. Betty recognized that the sadness she felt was clinical depression. Though it had to be hard for Moses and for Betty to face the difficult facts of the painful emotions they felt, Moses facing discouragement and insecurity, Betty facing depression, both found the courage and strength to *accurately assess themselves*. Both demonstrated *self-confidence and sureness about their self- worth and capabilities* by seeking help to restore themselves to their capabilities: Moses by acknowledging his concerns about his leadership and taking his concerns to God; Betty by defying social stigma to seek medical help for depression.

Conclusion

We are not born with self-awareness. We grow into it if we are intentional and fortunate to have role models like Moses and Betty. All of us, as we make life's journey, can learn, if we are willing, from those who have gone before. Moses and Betty are wonderful guides for us in how to be self-aware. Their self- awareness gave them sureness about their true self-worth and capabilities.[122] They heard the still, quiet voice of God, the "gut feeling," the gift from the Holy Spirit. This is a gift given to all of us.

If, as Daniel Goleman says, "awareness of one's own feelings as they occur is a keystone of emotional intelligence," Moses and Betty show genius EQs.

Questions For Thought And Reflection

1. God gently reminded Moses, in each of his concerns, that it was God who would be with him. It was God who would offer words. It was God who would offer the proof for people to see. It's all God and his work inside of us, teaching us that the self-awareness comes because of who he is, not who we are or fail to be. Again, it is the God image implanted in us that helps us turn our self-awareness toward him and begin to live like him.

   > We can approach the burning bush. He is there.
   > We can question our abilities. He created us and knows us.
   > We can work on ourselves. He shows us the way.
   > Have you ever sensed there is a new direction for your life? a "burning bush"? a "God nudge"?

2. What are the experiences that have brought you closer to your "burning bush" that tell you to come closer, or to run for the hills?

3. What do you think about Moses's candid conversations with God? Does this encourage you to do the same or do you feel God is far away?

4. Listening to the whisper of the Holy Spirit inside of us helps us to become more aware of God. Such listening turns our self-awareness into God-awareness. In this place, we can realize that God is in us, and we are in God. In short, the key to sounder personal decision-making is being attuned to the God-voice inside each of us. Are you listening?

5. Moses' self-awareness led to a new purpose in life for him. Might self-awareness lead you to a greater purpose? How? Why not?

CHAPTER NINE: FORGIVENESS

Forgiveness is one of those areas of life that we all experience in offering or withholding it, in receiving forgiveness or refusing it. This chapter discusses why and how forgiveness is a part of emotional intelligence. It looks at the forgiveness modeled by Jesus, then turns to behavioral science on the health benefits of forgiveness, what forgiveness is and is not, and the phases of forgiveness. The contemporary person we look at is Anthony Ray Hinton who spent thirty years on death row before he was freed by appellate courts and released. This chapter concludes by noting how the insights from behavioral science apply to the forgiveness modeled by Jesus and Ray Hinton.

Jesus And Those Whom He Forgave
Jesus did not just suggest or even command forgiveness; he demonstrated this powerful emotional intelligence trait. Let's look at two examples:

> *The Woman Who Wept at Jesus's Feet*
> "When one of the Pharisees invited Jesus to have dinner with him, he went to the Pharisee's house and reclined at the table. A woman in that town who lived a sinful life learned that Jesus was eating at the Pharisee's house, so she came there with an alabaster jar of perfume. As she stood behind him at his feet weeping, she began to wet his feet with her tears. Then she wiped them with her hair, kissed them and poured perfume on them.
> "When the Pharisee who had invited him saw this, he said to himself, 'If this man were a prophet, he would know who is touching him and what kind of woman she is—that she is a sinner.'
> "Jesus answered him, 'Simon, I have something to tell you.' 'Tell me, teacher,' he said. 'Two people owed money to a certain moneylender. One owed him five hundred denarii, and the other fifty. Neither of them had the money to pay him back, so he forgave the debts of both. Now which of them will love him more?'
> "Simon replied, 'I suppose the one who had the bigger debt forgiven.' 'You have judged correctly,' Jesus said. Then he turned toward the woman and said to Simon, 'Do you see this woman? I came into your house. You did not give me any water for my feet, but she wet my feet with her tears and wiped them with her

hair. You did not give me a kiss, but this woman, from the time I entered, has not stopped kissing my feet. You did not put oil on my head, but she has poured perfume on my feet. Therefore, I tell you, her many sins have been forgiven—as her great love has shown. But whoever has been forgiven little loves little.'

"Then Jesus said to her, 'Your sins are forgiven.' The other guests began to say among themselves, 'Who is this who even forgives sins?' Jesus said to the woman, 'Your faith has saved you; go in peace'" (Luke 7:36-50.)

The Paralyzed Man

"When Jesus again entered Capernaum, the people heard that he had come home. They gathered in such large numbers that there was no room left, not even outside the door, and he preached the word to them. Some men came, bringing to him a paralyzed man, carried by four of them. Since they could not get him to Jesus because of the crowd, they made an opening in the roof above Jesus by digging through it and then lowered the mat the man was lying on. When Jesus saw their faith, he said to the paralyzed man, 'Son, your sins are forgiven.'

"Now some teachers of the law were sitting there, thinking to themselves, 'Why does this fellow talk like that? He's blaspheming! Who can forgive sins but God alone?'

"Immediately Jesus knew in his spirit that this was what they were thinking in their hearts, and he said to them, 'Why are you thinking these things? Which is easier: to say to this paralyzed man, Your sins are forgiven, or to say, Get up, take your mat and walk? But I want you to know that the Son of Man has authority on earth to forgive sins.' So he said to the man, 'I tell you, get up, take your mat and go home.' He got up, took his mat and walked out in full view of them all. This amazed everyone and they praised God, saying, 'We have never seen anything like this!'" (Mark 2: 1-12).

These are the two instances in the Bible when Jesus expressly forgave another's sins. He often declared, "Your faith has made you well." He told the criminal beside him on Golgotha, "Today you will be with me in Paradise." He asked His Father to "forgive them for they know not what they do." But only in these two instances does Jesus invoke directly on another child of God the forgiveness of their sins.

Behavioral Science Of Forgiveness

How can we understand the act of forgiveness as part of emotional intelligence? Dr. Janet Shales wrote:

> "Choosing forgiveness embodies the essence of emotional intelligence. It requires self-, other- and social-awareness, as well as the capacity to move beyond one's present emotions to a more expansive state. Forgiveness, although often quite challenging, is a gift that you give to yourself — a gift that momentarily releases you from the past. The act of forgiveness requires letting go of something — a sense of injustice, disappointment, rage, perspective, desire, expectation, vision, and/or hope. Forgiveness requires moving beyond what should have been to a place of coexisting with what occurred. This does not in any way suggest that you should agree with, condone, or appreciate the action or situation that calls for your forgiveness, especially when faced with objectively dreadful situations that are out of your control and understanding."[123]

As Beverly Flanagan noted: "Forgiveness has nothing to do with forgetting. To forgive, one must remember the past, put it into perspective, and move beyond it. Without remembrance, no wound can be transcended."[124] Growing numbers of recent studies show the health benefits of forgiveness: "lowering the risk of heart attack; improving cholesterol levels and sleep; and reducing pain, blood pressure, and levels of anxiety, depression and stress."[125]

As Dr. Karen Swartz, director of the Mood Disorders Adult Consultation Clinic at The Johns Hopkins Hospital, noted: "There is an enormous physical burden to being hurt and disappointed. Chronic anger puts you into a fight-or-flight mode, which results in numerous changes in heart rate, blood pressure and immune response. Those changes, then, increase the risk of depression, heart disease, and diabetes among other conditions. Forgiveness, however, calms stress levels, leading to improved health."[126] Moreover, "the research points to an increase in the forgiveness — health connection as you age."[127]

According to Everett L. Worthington, Jr, there are three stages of forgiveness. First comes *anger and wanting revenge*. Acknowledging our anger at someone's sin against us is the first step in our own healing and wholeness. This acknowledgement and release can aid in our journey of emotional intelligence. The wrong against us is not removed, but the anger, hurt, and the emotional energy it takes to hang on to the anger begins to dissipate when we become willing to forgive. As long as we remain angry and want revenge, the anger of our unforgiveness festers and grows within us, extinguishing a part of our mental health.

The second stage of forgiveness is *decisional forgiveness* (*i.e.* I know it is bad for me to carry around such anger, so I will let it go). At this stage, we intellectually recognize that refusing to forgive and move on hurts one person: ourselves. We realize that it makes no sense to hold anger or to place blame for wrong done to us because that type of hoarding anger leads to our detriment. As long as we refuse to forgive, our transgressor retains power over us — to make us angry, sad, unwilling to move on. To forgive frees us to move on with our lives.

Obsessing about grudges results in rumination which is associated with mental disorders of anxiety, fear, depression, PTSD, and obsessive-compulsive disorders. Studies of rumination show that it is counterproductive for many reasons:

- requires emotional energy that we all need and can use elsewhere,
- gives the wrongdoer power over us long after the wrong has been done,
- causes stress and all of the physical and psychological problems that stress places on our bodies,
- impacts other relationships and our capacity to enjoy life,
- keeps us from growing as people which we all need to do to function as life throws more curve balls at us.[128]

Intellectually deciding that it would be a good idea (for us and our health) to forgive is one thing; actually forgiving another is a great deal harder. This is where the third stage of forgiveness, *emotional forgiveness*, comes in. Emotional forgiveness is forgiving another in our hearts, regardless of the benefit to ourselves. As Worthington says, "God requires decisional forgiveness of us; God desires emotional forgiveness."[129] And oh, the rewards. When we are able to emotionally forgive, we have more power to grow into the person God created us to be. [130] Jesus models the third stage of forgiveness in his words on the cross, "Forgive them, Father, for they know not what they do" (Luke 23:34). Not surprisingly perhaps, while the first two stages have some benefits to forgiving another for physical health, mental health, relational and spiritual health, most of the health benefits come through reducing our stress responses when we emotionally forgive.[131]

Anthony Ray Hinton

Anthony Ray Hinton grew up in rural Alabama. At age of 29, Ray, who worked the nightshift at a warehouse, was arrested on robbery and attempted murder charges after being misidentified by the manager of the Quincy restaurant where the robbery occurred. Despite the facts that Ray had an airtight alibi for when the crimes occurred (he was clocked in for his shift at the warehouse), had never been arrested for a violent crime, and passed a polygraph exam, he was arrested as the perpetrator of the Quincy restaurant robbery.

Investigators searched Ray's mother's home, where Ray lived, and found a 25-year-old .38 caliber pistol. They seized the pistol and presented at trial prosecution evidence from a ballistics examination stating that the pistol had been used in the Quincy restaurant robbery and shooting as well as in two prior restaurant robberies where the managers had been killed.[132] At trial, Ray was represented by an appointed attorney who on Ray's behalf selected as the defense ballistics expert witness a visually-impaired civil engineer with no expertise in firearms identification. This "expert witness" admitted while testifying that he could not operate the machinery necessary to examine the evidence. With no credible expert to challenge the state's assertion of a match, Ray was convicted and sentenced to death.[133]

Ray steadfastly maintained his innocence. After years of appeals, the U.S. Supreme Court unanimously overturned his conviction upon finding that Ray had ineffective assistance of counsel at trial. The court granted Ray a new trial. On remand from the U.S. Supreme Court, prosecutors admitted that the Alabama Department of Forensic Sciences had confirmed that the crime bullets could not be matched to the Hinton weapon. The ballistics evidence presented by the state earlier was wholly discredited by three highly qualified firearms examiners, including the former chief of the FBI's Firearm and Toolmarks Unit, who testified that the bullets from all three crimes could not be matched to a single gun at all, much less to Ray's mother's gun.[134]

After nearly thirty years in solitary confinement on Alabama's death row, Ray Hinton's conviction was set aside by appellate courts, and he was released from prison.

Was Ray angry when he was wrongfully convicted? Yes! he told us. He was "angry at God who he thought had abandoned him when he needed him the most." He was angry at the men who he believed had lied and conspired to take his life. As Ray told us, "I wanted to escape and choke the life out of those men."

After several years, though, Ray "looked in the mirror one morning and didn't like what I was looking at. I wasn't smiling, and I no longer was making others laugh." Ray realized at that moment that anger was silently killing him and that it had taken away his joy for life. "I refused to allow it any longer, so I prayed, 'God, I beg you to remove this hatred from around my heart. Restore to me the joy I once had.'" It took time but eventually, Ray's anger left, and his joy returned.

Ray told us, "I began to see that to be free, you have to forgive." He prayed to love the men he hated, "as his mother had taught him." He could hear his mother, who had passed away when he was in custody, saying to him, "You are not responsible for how others treat you, but you are responsible for how you treat others." And Ray prayed for "a heart of lovingkindness." Whereas before he had prayed for God's help in forgiving the men who had put him on death row, "so I could sleep good at night," now he prayed for the men "so that they could sleep at night."

The Ties That Bind: Forgiveness In Day-To-Day Life

Let's look at what Jesus and Ray Hinton can teach us. Note what Jesus taught about forgiveness when he encountered the woman who wept and the paralyzed man: that we are to forgive all sinners, whether they have committed many great sins, or a few lesser sins and that when we seek forgiveness, we do so with humility and honesty about ourselves and what we have done.

In the New Testament, the Greek verb *aphiemi* primarily means "to send away." By sending away the sins of the woman who wept and of the paralyzed man, Jesus freed them from the burden of their sins at that moment in their lives.

In these two stories, Jesus showed us the benefits of following his forgiving example. An old adage says, "Bitterness is the poison we take hoping someone else will die." Failing to forgive others leaves us little room for the joy that God intends for us to know. For "He came that we might have life and have it abundantly." What abundant life can we experience when we carry the weight of anger or resentment at another? Sending that away, emptying ourselves of that bitterness opens space for the joy for which we were created.

Ray Hinton traveled through the three stages of forgiveness. His life shows how that made him free. At first, Ray experienced the anger, resentment, and a thirst for vengeance of which Worthington speaks. After several years, realizing that his anger at others was silently killing him, Ray reached *decisional* forgiveness. It was then that he realized that in order to be truly free of hatred, he had to go beyond giving up anger. Ray prayed for a heart of lovingkindness.

Ray reached *emotional forgiveness* not because of what forgiving his accusers would do for him, but because he genuinely wanted those he had resented for so long to have peace. Traveling the three stages of forgiveness made him free. When the prosecutor from Ray's trial died years later, Ray prayed that the prosecutor would find peace in heaven. Ray was released from prison after thirty years, but it was not just that release that made him free; it was acknowledging his hatred, making the decision to forgive, and truly forgiving others, in his heart, not just in his head.

Conclusion

Jesus and Ray teach us lessons about forgiveness. We close this chapter with Jesus' ultimate lesson: "When they came to the place called Galgatha, the Skull, there they crucified him and the criminals, one on the right and the other on the left. But Jesus was saying, 'Father, forgive them for they do not know what they are doing.'"[135] Even on the cross, Jesus asked his Father to forgive those who were killing him. Forgiving those who don't ask for or don't deserve forgiveness: this is true emotional intelligence. As Ray Hinton shows us, this is the forgiveness that sets us free.

Questions For Thought And Reflection

1. What does the world teach about forgiveness?

2. Who might you need to forgive? How often have you been forgiven? Are there things for which you need to forgive yourself?

3. Are justice, mercy, and forgiveness related? How?

4. Was there justice in the stories we read? Did the guests at Simon's house believe that Jesus should have forgiven the woman who wept? Did the people at Capernaum agree that Jesus had the authority to forgive the paralyzed man? Should those that led to Ray Hinton's wrongful conviction be forgiven…or sanctioned? Is there justice in forgiveness? Does it matter?

5. According to Aristotle, "Anyone can become angry — that is easy. But to be angry with the right person, to the right degree, at the right time, for the right purpose, and in the right way — this is not easy."[136] How did Ray Hinton redirect his anger? How might we redirect our anger "in the right way"?

6. Try praying daily for the person you are forgiving and notice over time the effect that those prayers have on the success of your forgiveness.

CHAPTER TEN: EMPATHY

The English word *empathy* derives from the Greek word *empatheia* which means "feeling into." Empathy is the ability to perceive the subjective experiences of another person, which is associated with being well adjusted and connected to other people. We look at how Jesus taught empathy by his deeds and teachings, and at the work of John Dorsey, a psychiatrist in rural Alabama.

Those Whom Jesus Helped
Let us look at Jesus's empathy in the feeding of the five thousand:

> *"Jesus crossed to the far shore of the Sea of Galilee and a great crowd of people followed him because they saw the signs he had performed by healing the sick. Then Jesus went up on a mountainside and sat down with his disciples. When Jesus looked up and saw a great crowd coming toward him, he said to Philip, 'Where shall we buy bread for these people to eat?' He asked this only to test him, for he already had in mind what he was going to do.*
>
> *"Philip answered him, 'It would take more than half a year's wages to buy enough bread for each one to have a bite!' Another of his disciples, Andrew, Simon Peter's brother, spoke up, 'Here is a boy with five small barley loaves and two small fish, but how far will they go among so many?'*
>
> *"Jesus said, 'Have the people sit down.' There was plenty of grass in that place, and they sat down (about five thousand men were there). Jesus then took the loaves, gave thanks, and distributed to those who were seated as much as they wanted. He did the same with the fish.*
>
> *"When they had all had enough to eat, he said to his disciples, 'Gather the pieces that are left over. Let nothing be wasted.' So they gathered them and filled twelve baskets with the pieces of the five barley loaves left over by those who had eaten"(John 6:1-13).*

Despite being tired and needing rest, Jesus rose to teach the crowd that had followed him. When they were hungry, Jesus did not tell them to go home but with compassion for them, set forth a plan to feed everyone. Aware that the large crowd was restless, he first calmed everyone. Second, he gave thanks. Then he distributed the food that had been gathered. Was it by his example and that of the little boy who shared his few loaves and fishes, that others learned empathy, which brought forth the ability of others to share food they may have with them?

On another occasion, Jesus demonstrated empathy for a person scorned by synagogue leaders:

> *"On a sabbath Jesus was teaching in one of the synagogues, and a woman was there who had been crippled by a spirit for eighteen years. She was bent over and could not straighten up at all. When Jesus saw her, he called her forward and said to her, 'Woman, you are set free from your infirmity.' Then he put his hands on her, and immediately she straightened up and praised God.*
>
> *"Indignant because Jesus had healed on the sabbath, the synagogue leader said to the people, 'There are six days for work. So come and be healed on those days, not on the sabbath.' The Lord answered him, 'You hypocrites! Doesn't each of you on the sabbath untie your ox or donkey from the stall and lead it out to give it water? Then should not this woman, a daughter of Abraham, whom Satan has kept bound for eighteen long years, be set free on the sabbath day from what bound her?'*
>
> *"When he said this, all his opponents were humiliated, but the people were delighted with all the wonderful things he was doing"* (Luke 13:10-17).

In this story, Jesus seemed to know and understand this woman's pain without a word passing between them. He called her to him and healed her, not because she asked but because of his empathy towards her. Imagine what this woman's life had been like. She had walked for years face down. She had withstood ridicule from those who did not understand. Imagine how difficult life's duties were for her. Surely, she wanted to stand straight and tall and look into the eyes of those around her. But she was burdened by this disease; it caused her pain, made her feel awkward, embarrassed her.

The empathy of Jesus in this story is extraordinary. He noticed this woman. He had eyes to see her. She wasn't just a handicapped person in the temple that day, someone to dismiss quickly. He saw her, really saw her. Jesus seemed not interested in anything but her pain of eighteen years.

A woman two thousand years ago in the temple being called by a teacher is an incredible story. Here Jesus was courageous enough to be empathetic despite the disapproval his kindness toward this woman brought from the synagogue leaders.

Think of those individuals you have seen who are bent over from disease or burdens, of the times in your life when you felt bent over from the burdens you have carried. We all can feel bent over with responsibilities and overwhelmed with sadness about things going on in our lives. We can all feel bowed down with the weight of the things that go wrong in the world and that good people, on opposite sides of the political spectrum, see so differently. But as Jesus taught, we can stand up straight in our souls. Jesus's lessons in empathy can straighten the bent-over places in our lives.

Behavioral Science On Empathy
Empathy is "the ability to know how another feels."[137] The benefits of being empathetic begin early:

> "Children who showed an aptitude for reading feelings nonverbally were among the most popular in their schools and the most emotionally stable. They did better in school, even though, on average, their IQs were not higher than those of children who were less skilled at reading nonverbal messages." [138]

People who are empathetic often are "social magnets." These individuals reflect their genuine empathy, making others feel comfortable, accepted, wanted. This is because genuine emotions are contagious. As Daniel Goleman explained, we unconsciously imitate the emotions we see displayed by someone else. The mood of the more emotionally expressive person transfers to the more passive one.[139]

Richard Wiseman, a research professor of psychology at the University of Hertfordshire in Britain, has studied "social magnets," finding that such individuals benefit from their empathetic nature.[140] They are "effective at building secure and long-lasting attachments with people they meet. They are easy to get to know, and most people like them. They tend to be trusting and form close relationships with others."[141] Interestingly, social magnets exhibit body language and facial expressions that convey empathy and openness to others. They smile much more than most of us and engage in far more eye contact. They engage in "open body language: uncrossing their arms and legs, pointing their bodies toward the person to whom they are speaking, and gesture using open palms." [142]

In short, empathy "comes into play in a vast array of life arenas, from sales and management to ... parenting, to compassion and political action."[143] The enormous benefits of empathy have been shown: "In tests with over seven thousand people in the United States and eighteen other countries, the benefits of being able to read feelings from nonverbal cues included being better adjusted emotionally, more popular, more outgoing, and perhaps not surprisingly, more sensitive."[144]

Let us look at John Dorsey, a physician who through his empathy brings a new meaning to healing.

John Dorsey

If you asked John Dorsey when he was a medical student what he would be doing when he completed his training, it is doubtful he would have said living and practicing in the rural South. John Dorsey had a circuitous route to Greene County, Alabama. He received his BA in Neurosciences from Pomona College, his MD from the Sydney Kimmel Medical College in Philadelphia, and his MBA with a focus on Health and Medical Services Administration from Widener University.

After completing his residency in psychiatry in California, John served on the faculty at a medical center in Los Angeles where he was co-medical director of a team that provided psychiatric and supportive services to more than one hundred patients with severe mental illness living in southern California. He also served as a staff psychiatrist at a facility that provided mental health services to severely mentally ill and homeless individuals in Los Angeles County.

In 2005, John felt a call to move to a smaller community with a more personal way of living and practicing psychiatry. After meeting a colleague who hailed from Alabama at a psychiatry conference and who encouraged him to consider the south, John accepted a position with Bryce Hospital, the state mental health institution for Alabama located in Tuscaloosa. John thought that this would give him an opportunity to get his feet planted and to get to know the state a little better as he made the transition from California to Alabama.

When John was enroute to Tuscaloosa to accept the Bryce Hospital position with his car packed with all of his belongings, John's plans were thrown into turmoil. First, he got a call, while driving through

Oklahoma, that his job with Bryce fell through. Second, Hurricane Katrina hit, and travel through the south became virtually impossible.

Struggling and lost and not knowing anybody, John decided nonetheless to proceed. Evacuees filled every hotel room in West Alabama. As John drove from place to place searching for lodging, he saw a sign in the small town of Moundville south of Tuscaloosa: "Mobile Homes Sales Office." He pulled over and went into the office to inquire whether they would consider renting him a mobile home. Understandably, John was met with skepticism on the part of the sales manager because of his California license plate, different accent, and long hair. "I think they thought I was going to start a meth lab…or worse!" Nevertheless, he convinced the sales director of his authenticity, so he rented a mobile home to him and gave him a couple of contacts in the nearby town of Greensboro, and off John went.

In Greensboro, Alabama, John discovered a community that had been extremely prosperous before the Civil War but that had struggled economically over the last fifty years. Greene County is one of the poorest counties in one of the poorest states in the United States. Despite its poverty, John found Greene County "such a rich and complex place" with what he was looking for: "a strong sense of community, deep roots in the past, a strong sense of people wanting to help one another out." As John says, "I really love being in a small town. I love personal relationships. I love to be able to feel like I'm making an impact and contributing to the community." And what an impact he is making!

John began working at the local community mental health center and then at a local hospital that had recently opened a geriatric psychiatry unit. "I've always had a desire to take care of people living with mental illness," John said. While working in California, he saw the challenges that people with mental illness face. In Greensboro, John had a chance "to combine good psychiatric care with the extra support people living with mental illness need to help live well and more successfully in their community."

The Ties That Bind:
Empathy In Day-To-Day Life: Empathy Through Action
Empathy is one of the fundamental lessons Jesus gave us. The feeding of the five thousand and Jesus's reaching out to the bent-over woman are but two of the many instances when Jesus demonstrated empathy

through his actions. Throughout the gospels, Jesus demonstrates empathy in action for people who were "sheep without a shepherd" (Mark 6:34), who were in distress (John 11:33-35, Luke 7:13), who were hungry (John 6:15). John Dorsey has put his empathy into action. In 2007, two years after arriving in Greene County, John started an after-school program for at-risk students at Greensboro Elementary School.

Today, the project has grown to more than seventy students per day in grades K-12.

Through his work, John had seen "the lack of really sufficient structure for people to make the transition out of the hospital and also to avoid ending up back in the hospital or in an institutional setting." In 2009, seeing the chance "to combine good psychiatric care with the extra support people living with mental illness need to help live well and more successfully in their community," John created *Project Horseshoe Farm*.

Project Horseshoe Farm provides an independent living housing program for women, especially those living with mental illness. The project's goal is to "help support residents' health and quality of life and help them to live the most independent life they can." *Project Horseshoe Farm* is housed in a beautiful turn-of-the-century Victorian country home that John bought and restored with community support. This first enhanced independent living housing program has spawned two other houses run by *Project Horseshoe Farm* which together can accommodate up to thirteen women. Over the years, many women have successfully transitioned back to their families or independent living.

In 2018, *Project Horseshoe Farm* expanded to include a community center in downtown Greensboro with scheduled morning programs for seniors, adults living with mental illness, or anyone who wants to come by to enjoy fellowship and good fun. About 25-50 adults from all over the area congregate each day at the center for a range of social activities, health and wellness, and other programs. The center also includes a mental health clinic which John staffs as the psychiatrist, a primary care medical clinic, and a community garden, laundry facilities, and a large state-of-the-art kitchen for anyone to use.

To help keep *Project Horseshoe Farm* operational, it applies to foundations for grants, and churches and individuals have stepped up. Always evolving, Horseshoe Farm has launched a successful second location in Marion, Alabama, and is looking to replicate its model more broadly across the country. It also has launched a "Farming, Health, and Nutrition" track to its Fellowship program and developed close ties with the local Hale County Hospital as well as with the Auburn University Rural Studio architecture program and medical and health professions programs from around the state.

The Ties That Bind: *Empathy Through Teaching*

Jesus taught empathy, often through parables. Think, for example, of Jesus's parable of the good Samaritan. When a lawyer (who sought to "justify himself" in front of the others) asked Jesus, "Who is my neighbor?" Jesus replied with a parable:

> *A man was going down from Jerusalem to Jericho, and fell into the hands of robbers, who stripped him, beat him, and went away, leaving him half dead. Now by chance a priest was going down that road; and when he saw him, he passed by on the other side. So likewise a Levite, when he came to the place and saw him, passed by on the other side. But a Samaritan while traveling came near him; and when he saw him, he was moved with pity. He went to him and bandaged his wounds, having poured oil and wine on them. Then he put him on his own animal, brought him to an inn, and took care of him. The next day he took out two denarii, gave them to the innkeeper, and said, 'Take care of him; and when I come back, I will repay you whatever more you spend.' Which of these three, do you think, was a neighbor to the man who fell into the hands of the robbers?' He said, 'The one who showed him mercy.' Jesus said to him, 'Go and do likewise.' (Luke 10: 30-37).*

In this parable, two esteemed members of the community, the priest and the Levite, showed complete lack of empathy to a person in need, while another, a Samaritan, viewed by society as a pariah, "was moved to pity." It was the Samaritan, not the esteemed members of the community, who took care of the man. The Samaritan knew who his neighbor was. Did Jesus' parable allow the lawyer to see for himself who was his neighbor?

Jesus' parables demonstrated thousands of years ago what modern scholarship shows: that empathy can be taught more effectively by calling attention to the distress our misbehavior causes another than by telling us we have done something wrong.[145] As Jesus' parable of the good Samaritan so aptly demonstrates, parables allow the listener to emphasize with those in the parable and perhaps to grow in their own empathy. Jesus likely learned the power of parables from Jewish tradition. Many of the Old Testament prophets taught by parable. Note for example, Nathan's confrontation of King David after he ordered the murder of Uriah, husband of Bathsheba, whom David wanted for a wife:

> [Nathan] came to him, and said to him, 'There were two men in a certain city, the one rich and the other poor. The rich man had very many flocks and herds; but the poor man had nothing but one little ewe lamb, which he had bought. He brought it up, and it grew up with him and with his children; it used to eat of his meager fare, and drink from his cup, and lie in his bosom, and it was like a daughter to him. Now there came a traveler to the rich man, and he was loath to take one of his own flock or herd to prepare for the wayfarer who had come to him, but he took the poor man's lamb and prepared that for the guest who had come to him.
>
> Then David's anger was greatly kindled against the man. He said to Nathan, 'As the Lord lives, the man who has done this deserves to die; he shall restore the lamb fourfold, because he did this thing, and because he had no pity.' Nathan said to David, 'You are the man!' (1 Samuel 1-7).

As the Reverend Dr. John Claypool has said, a parable is a painting that becomes a mirror. With this parable to King David, Nathan painted a picture that became a mirror in which David could see himself. David saw the tragedy his misbehavior caused someone else.

"Mirroring" is a standard practice used today by therapists to teach empathy. Like the parables, "mirroring therapy" allows us to hear our actions from the perspective of another person. Daniel Goleman explains mirroring therapy: "One method for effective emotional listening, called 'mirroring,' is commonly used in marital therapy. When one partner makes a complaint, the other repeats it back in her own words, trying to capture not just the thought but also the feelings that go with it. The partner mirroring checks with the other to be sure the restatement is on target, and if not, tries again until it is right — something that seems simple but is surprisingly tricky in execution. The effect of being mirrored accurately is not just feeling understood but having the added sense of being in emotional attunement."[146]

Like our master teacher who knew best how to teach empathy, John teaches empathy to those he trains. In 2009, John added a fellowship program for top recent college graduates who are interested in a "gap year" before heading on to medical or other graduate school. The fellows spend one year with *Horseshoe Farm* helping manage and lead all of *Horseshoe Farm*'s programs and initiatives. In its inaugural year, the fellows program had three fellows. Today, it has grown to a current class of 21 fellows. Large numbers of students apply from all over the country to serve as *Project Horseshow Farm* fellows. Over the last ten years, more than ninety fellows have participated in the program, with the majority going on to medical school, other health professions, public health, law, or other graduate programs after their experience. Many who go on to medical school choose to pursue a rural track.

The course curriculum for the fellows, created by John, serves as the basis for the fellows' weekly discussions. The curriculum's focus is on citizenship, community, health systems, leadership and management, community health, and effectively turning ideas into action. As John says, "We believe that a generation of students stands ready and eager to build a better future in healthcare, in education, and in communities across our nation, and we are working very hard at Horseshoe Farm to provide direction, teaching, and support to help them fulfill this mission."

Conclusion

Jesus and John Dorsey embody empathy. They demonstrate profound compassion for others (Mark 6:34, Matthew 14:14, Luke 7:14), care for the needs of others (John 6:15) and are deeply moved in spirit and are troubled by the plight of others (John 11:33). The stories of feeding the five thousand, the good Samaritan, the bent over woman, and *Project Horseshoe Farm* show how Jesus and John set empathy as their north star. They embody how to turn empathy into action, how to have eyes to see and ears to hear those hurting in our world.

Jesus's coming to Earth is the greatest act of empathy in history. Because of Jesus's birth, death, and resurrection, God now sees as humans see, feels as humans feel, thinks as humans think. (Hebrews 2:16-18). God knows what life is like because he came right inside life in Jesus.

John's heart goes out to those who are hurting from grief, distress, poverty, and mental illness. As a psychiatrist and a person of compassion, he is able to read others' emotional cues. He loves his neighbor as himself, figuratively, sometimes literally, picking up the sick on the side of the road. He teaches by his deeds and to those he trains. And his joy is contagious. John Dorsey is a twenty-first-century embodiment of empathy. As one friend and colleague of John's in Greene County, told us, "God sent John."[147]

Questions For Thought And Reflection

1. In the story of the good Samaritan and Jesus with the bent-over woman, it seems that the leaders of the day had difficulty with the practice of empathy, that those who may not "walk in the church's way" are unworthy of compassion. Are there ways we limit ourselves in feeling or expressing empathy?

2. How is empathy accepted, respected, and encouraged in the world today? What may be the reasons for that? What can we do in our day-to-day lives about that?

3. What are some of the reasons that we fail to act or notice those who need our empathy?

4. Do you notice that your family or friends seek your empathy? What are some ways you can turn your empathy into action for your family and friends?

5. Are you bent over? How would you feel to be able to stand up and have your burden lifted? Do you know someone who is bent over? How might you help that person, even for a moment, to have their burden lifted?

6. Is there a relationship between empathy and morality? Consider Daniel Goleman: The roots of morality are in empathy, since sharing distress moves people to act to help. The more empathetic people are, the more they will favor the moral principle that resources should be shared.[148] What do you think?

CHAPTER ELEVEN: STRENGTHS AND WEAKNESSES, KNOWING WHAT THEY ARE AND HOW TO MANAGE THEM

This chapter focuses on the emotional intelligence skill of recognizing our strengths and building upon them, recognizing our weaknesses and finding "work arounds" for them. We look at the life of Job in the Old Testament and of Demarcus Joiner, a young man who survived kidney cancer at the age of five to become one of the youngest and most inspiring leaders in the state of Alabama.

Job

Job, a good and righteous person, was prosperous and well-liked and respected in his community. Then, suddenly, with one tragedy after another, he loses all he has. It is then that we see one of Job's strengths: his confidence and self-assurance. Job continued believing in a good and loving God even when his faith was tested by disasters that befell him:

> *"There was once a man in the land of Uz whose name was Job. That man was blameless and upright, one who feared God and turned away from evil. In one day, Job loses everything: his oxen, donkeys, sheep, camels, servants, all of his sons and daughters, and his health: Loathsome sores [sprung up] on Job from the sole of his foot to the crown of his head." (Job1:1)*

Job's wife and friends seek to advise him, urging him to repent for what he, Job, had done to bring about his calamities. Job's wife said to him," *Do you still persist in your integrity? Curse God and die,*" and Job answered, "*Shall we receive the good at the hand of God, and not receive the bad?*" Job's friends insisted that Job should cease his evil deeds since his bad fortunes were because God was punishing him for them: *"If iniquity is in your hand, put it far away, and do not let wickedness reside in your tents."* They advised Job to repent: *If you will seek God and make supplication to the Almighty... surely then he will rouse himself for you and restore to you your rightful place."*

Job's family and friends, like most people of that time and place, believed that hardships in life were punishments imposed by a vengeful God. As the Reverend Dr. John Claypool describes, this view, prevalent at the time, was a "simple equation" that one was prosperous if righteous and suffered if sinful.

Job resisted his family's and friends' view of God. He told them that their view of God was wrong, that good and evil are part of life; they are not rewards or punishments bestowed by a vengeful God: *"Your maxims are proverbs of ashes"* (Job 13:12); *"Those who plow iniquity and sow trouble reap the same. Do not human beings have a hard service on earth and are not their days like the days of a laborer...[W]e are all "allotted months of emptiness, and nights of mercy"* (Job 7:1-3). Job argued that God stands with us in our turmoil's sharing our pain and offering us strength for our journey: *"For I know that my redeemer lives and that I... shall see God whom I shall see on my side and my ears shall behold."* (Job 19:25-26)

In resisting the temptation of his wife and friends (and reflected in many voices of the Old Testament) to view God as vengeful, inflicting punishment, pain, and suffering on human beings, Job foreshadows the message Jesus brings centuries later: that God is just and merciful and loves with abundant grace and that sometimes bad things happen no matter what we do, yet God forgives us, suffers with us, and is with us in our suffering. By holding fast to his view of God in the face of adversity and different views by his family and friends, Job shows self-assurance. As such, he was able to see and build upon opportunities that came for him to rebuild a new life.

Behavioral Science Of Managing Strengths And Weaknesses: Play To Your Long Suit

Strengths are the "natural talents and personality traits that remain relatively stable throughout life."[149] All of us have innate strengths. Emotional intelligence is the ability to identify our strengths and seek paths in life that allow us to use them, in other words, to "play to our long suit."

Studies show that those individuals who engage in activities that call upon their strengths display more confidence, direction, hope, and kindness toward others, are more engaged in life, do a better job of whatever they undertake, and are more likely to report having an excellent quality of life in general. [150]

To maximize our strengths, we need to use them regularly. This is true whatever our level of natural talent. The most successful people start with dominant talent — and then add skills, knowledge, and practice. When they do so, their raw talent actually serves as a *multiplier*."[151] As Mihaly Csikszenthihalyi notes: "Only through extensive investments of psychic energy can a child with musical gifts turn into a musician, or a mathematically gifted child into an engineer or physicist."[152]

We all have weaknesses, areas of life which are difficult for us. To manage our weaknesses, studies show we are better off learning to work around them rather than focusing time and energy into improving them. If I am terrible at directions, my time and effort is better spent learning all I can about GPS, not getting lost all the time. If I am socially anxious my energy is better spent learning how to engage with others in small groups, or one-on-one, or developing a gracious exit strategy for large social events, rather than forcing myself to be a social butterfly.

Longitudinal studies following young children into their adult years show that "the key to human development is building on who we already are,"[153] rather than focusing on shoring up areas of weakness. "While it may be possible, with a considerable amount of work, to add talent where little exists, …research suggests that this may not be the best use of [our]time."[154]

The problem is that while we all would like to choose life paths that allow us to rely on our areas of strength rather than on our areas of weakness, few of us "have the luxury to simply stop doing necessary tasks just because we aren't naturally good at them."[155] Thus, we need to know how to manage life when called upon to operate in our areas of weakness. We can do so by establishing "workarounds, which are systems to manage our lesser talent and keep things on track." [156]

We now turn to our modern-day hero, Demarcus Joiner, who like Job, faced a life-threating setback. Like Job, Demarcus also demonstrates self-assurance in finding and relying upon his strengths and developing workarounds to manage his weaknesses.

Demarcus
Demarcus Joiner grew up in Roanoke, Alabama, a town of 6,000. Demarcus's only sibling is his fraternal twin. As boys, Demarcus and his brother were, in Demarcus's words, "wild boys, tearing through the

house and playing outside all day." When they were in kindergarten, the boys were taken for a routine checkup. A few hours later, Demarcus was on his way to children's hospital in Atlanta, Georgia, to have a kidney removed. He had kidney cancer.

Hospitalized for weeks and confined to his home for months thereafter, Demarcus missed the rest of his kindergarten year. When he returned to school, some of the other kids saw the scar that went across his abdomen and asked what happened. Not wanting attention or sympathy, Demarcus told them that his cat scratched him. After his kidney removal, Demarcus was restricted from playing sports. This was a big disappointment because he loved playing sports and sports were much of what was available for kids to do in Roanoke, plus his twin brother, from whom he had been inseparable, continued to play sports.

By third grade, however, Demarcus began discovering talents he did not know he had. Good at music, he learned to play saxophone and participated in marching band and concert band, serving as drum major throughout high school. Gifted with a beautiful voice, Demarcus sang at church and with a choral group throughout college. Demarcus learned that he was a natural leader. He was elected "king" of his elementary school and a member of student council and/or president of his class every year throughout high school. Chosen to represent his school at the Boys State Leadership Program and Capstone Leadership Program while in high school, he met leaders throughout Alabama.

After high school, Demarcus attended the University of Alabama. Planning to major in political science, he majored in civil engineering because that was where scholarships were available. He performed in the Afro-American Gospel Choir and was elected to the Student Government Association (SGA), first as a senator for the College of Engineering and then as president. The SGA has a long and distinguished history at the University of Alabama, often serving as the "training ground" for future national and state leaders. SGA presidents have served as U.S. Senators and U.S. representatives, governors, and multiple state and municipal elected offices. One former SGA president even played with the New York Yankees alongside Babe Ruth and Lou Gehrig! Rare in the history of the SGA, Demarcus was unopposed when he ran for SGA president.

As a student leader at the University of Alabama, Demarcus demonstrated creativity, tenacity, organizational skills, hard work, and team building. As vice-president for Diversity and Inclusion, he organized the first Diversity and Inclusion Certification program at UA (securing funding, support, and dozens of speakers and panels). He initiated the first International Karaoke contest (international students at UA performing songs from their home countries all over the world) and helped inaugurate and organize the first Miss Unique UA pageant at the University of Alabama (a pageant spotlighting UA disabled women's beauty and confidence). As president of the SGA during the covid pandemic lockdown, Demarcus, often the only person in the empty, multi-story student center on a deserted campus, had to invent as he went. With the covid pandemic in full force and the 40,000 student campus closed, dorms evacuated, and all classes converted, overnight, to remote learning, the SGA was often the center of the storm, serving as a major communication hub for students and their families, handling thousands of questions and concerns.

Demarcus' journey shows something fundamental about emotional intelligence. We learn EQ skills by being in community with others. Demarcus's first and foremost community is his family. He credits his parents with teaching him how to prepare for difficulties. When he was in high school and planning to try out for drum major, his mother asked, "Have you practiced?" When he admitted he had not, she encouraged him to wait until the next year to try out when he had had time to practice. He followed her advice. When Demarcus told his mom that he wanted to be a public speaker, she said, "Then you have to practice enunciating." From these words of wisdom, Demarcus learned to plan, to anticipate, to prepare — exactly what he does with his calming rituals. When he got cancer, Demarcus's parents showed him how to handle adversities by their behavior: "My parents never got frazzled, never got down and no matter how bad or how well things went, their attitude was and continues to be, let's keep going." And that is how Demarcus deals with his life — he keeps on going.

Demarcus attended law school at the University of Alabama School of Law after graduating from the university and now practices law with a nationally known law firm.

The Ties That Bind: How We Can Manage Our
Strengths And Weaknesses In Day-To-Day Life
Both Job and Demarcus serve as excellent role models of individuals who know and use their strengths. They have similar strengths, one

of which is self-assurance, which is: "Confidence not just in your abilities but in your judgment. When you look at the world, you know that your perspective is unique and distinct. And because no one sees exactly what you see, you know that no one can make decisions for you."[157] Let us look at how they each demonstrated this confidence in themselves, and in who God is. Job displayed self-assurance as he resisted the certainty by his wife and friends that God had caused the tragedies that befell him. Job stood up to them and remained assured in his belief that God is good and loving, that God was not punishing him, and that God was present in Job's life, in sorrow and joy, and always would be.

Demarcus demonstrated the strength of self-assurance. Throughout his life many have given him advice, but Demarcus has followed the road which "felt right to me, not what others urge upon me." Demarcus works intentionally to discern "what direction to go in life." As he says, "I have so many people telling me what to do. I want to follow God's plan for me. Cancer taught me that what I thought was my next step was not what God thought." To hear God's guidance, Demarcus prays and "fasts from social media, going places or particular foods, sometimes," he adds with a smile, "even giving up Dr. Pepper."

Both Job and Demarcus demonstrate the strength of adaptability (discussed in more detail in the next chapter). Adaptability is the ability to pivot, to "adjust to a variety of different circumstances"; it is "essential to enjoying a happy, satisfying life." [158] Job demonstrated adaptability when his life hit one calamity after another. He adapted to his losses and moved on with an attitude of acceptance and openness for what lay ahead. Simillarly, throughout his life, Demarcus demonstrated adaptability. When kidney cancer ended all activities he loved, he found new passions — in music, leadership and service. When not selected for membership in a competitive organization in college, he ran for student office. When serving as an SGA officer, he often adapted, changing quickly to meet new circumstances whether it was a last-minute cancellation from a keynote speaker or a global pandemic. Like Job, Demarcus learned how to be adaptable from adversity: "When I got kidney cancer, I saw that anything can happen in the spur of the moment."

Note how both Job and Demarcus dealt with their weaknesses. Job had difficulty managing his negative emotions when his life shattered. He was, at times, overcome by anger, fear, exhaustion, and self-pity, wailing, "*I loathe my life*" (Job 9:21); "*My spirit is broken, my days are extinct*" (Job 17:1). He expressed pure anger at God: "*Did you not pour me out like milk and curdle me like cheese?*" (Job 10:10), "*Why did you bring me forth from the womb?*" (Job 10:18). Yet Job did not let his emotions derail him. He talked with his friends and even though he rejected their solutions, conversations with them strengthened his sense of God as present and powerful in his life. Job's railings at God may have, like a good cry, cleansed his emotional turmoil, calmed him, and allowed him to see God even more deeply than before calamities struck: "*I have heard of thee by the hearing of the ear: But now mine eye seeth thee.*" (Job 42:5); "*I know that you can do all things*" (Job 42:2).

Demarcus showed considerable emotional intelligence in identifying and managing his weaknesses. He told us that he was at his weakest when he "got tired but still had many commitments." On some days as SBA president, he had as many as sixteen meetings. And that was on top of being a full-time college student! Like Job who learned to manage his weaknesses, to purge his negative emotions by talking with family, friends, and God, Demarcus has developed strategies to help him manage his overcommitments and exhaustion. He engages in "calming rituals." As Demarcus explains: "Every night I carve out quiet time and every morning I put on gospel music first thing. He also intentionally "puts on a happy face," no matter how tired or discouraged he is because "It's not someone else's fault I'm tired."

Both Demarcus's and Job's journeys show us something else about using strengths and managing weaknesses. Their weaknesses are "shadow sides" of their strengths. Demarcus's weakness — getting tired but still having commitments to which he must attend — is a "shadow side" of his strength of leadership. Leaders are often overextended yet must carry on. Similarly, Job's weakness — becoming overwhelmed by disturbing emotions — is the "shadow side" of being human. Everyone, no matter how privileged, protected, wealthy, famous, or strong, will be overwhelmed by disturbing emotions at times. That is part of the human journey.

Conclusion

Like Job, like Demarcus, we all have strengths and weaknesses. Owning them, seeking out directions in life where we can use and build upon our strengths, and establishing workarounds for our weaknesses, is being emotionally intelligent.

Thoughts And Questions For Reflection

1. What are your strengths? How do you use them? Do you have some strengths you do not use? What are they and might you want to make changes in your life so you can use them more?

2. Are your strengths also the things you enjoy doing? Why might that make sense?

3. What are your areas of weakness? What "work arounds" have you developed to manage them? What additional workarounds might you develop?

4. Can you look back upon your life, especially as a young person growing up, and see evidence of your strengths and weaknesses at an early age?

5. Note that both Job and Demarcus lost what they, what all of us, may consider to be entitlements: good health, a strong family, reaping the benefits of hard work. The Reverend Dr. John Claypool talks about this sense of entitlement regarding things we have, that we feel we have earned. He suggests that the book of Job reminds us that the things we may become indignant about losing never belonged to us in the first place. We are not entitled to good health. We are not entitled to the bounty of a successful career. We are not entitled to a healthy, loving family. These, Claypool says, are gifts: "gifts beyond our deserving, graciously given to us by Another and thus not to be possessed or held onto as if they were ours." For us "to be angry because a gift has been taken away," Claypool says, "is to miss the whole point of life. That we have the things we cherish is more than we deserve. Gratitude and humility rather than resentment should characterize our handling of life."[159]

Do Job and Demarcus model John Claypool's vision of gifts given by God? Are there losses in your life, like in Job's, in Demarcus's, that are also gifts?

CHAPTER TWELVE: ADAPTABILITY

This chapter focuses on the emotional intelligence of adaptability: how we handle change, juggle life's demands, and approach new situations with fresh ideas.[160] It looks at the story of Ruth and Naomi in the Old Testament, and the life of Andrea Edmonds and her daughter, Ruthie.

Ruth And Naomi

The book of Ruth tells a story of "how we should live so as to be open to God's blessing." [161] It is "acknowledged as one of the finest stories in the Hebrew scriptures." [162] It is also a story about those who adapt well to change: Elimelech, a father and husband who moved his young family to a foreign land to obtain better living conditions; Naomi and her daughter-in-law, Ruth, who prevailed against all odds; Boaz who went against cultural norms to marry a foreign woman.

The book of Ruth was written between the sixth and fourth centuries BCE, "the time of judges" (referring to the governing structure of society). It begins in the land of Judah, "a simple agricultural economy that often necessitated emigration when the seasonal rains failed."[163] Elimelech and his family were among the many Judaeans who faced starvation during one of the seasons of drought and famine that struck Judah. To survive, they, like others, migrated to a neighboring land, Moab:

> *"In the days when the judges ruled, there was a famine in the land and a certain man of Bethlehem in Judah went to live in the country of Moab, he and his wife and two sons. The name of the man was Elimelech and the name of his wife Naomi and the names of his two sons were Mahlon and Chilion; they were Ephrathites from Bethlehem in Judah. They went into the country of Moab and remained there" (Ruth 1:1-3).*

It could not have been an easy decision for Elimelech to move his family to Moab. Not only were they leaving their homeland, extended families, and community, they were moving to a land at odds with their culture: "*According to Israel's religious and historical tradition the Moabites were 'the decedents of deception and incest.'*"[164] Tragically, Elimelech died after their move, leaving Naomi with two sons. The sons grew up and married Moabite women, but before children were born to either marriage, both sons died:

> "Elimelech and his family remained in Moab for a number of years. But Elimelech the husband of Naomi, died, and she was left with her two sons. These took Moabite wives; the name of the one was Orpah and the name of the other Ruth. When they had lived there about ten years both sons, Mahlon and Chilion, also died, so that the woman was left without her two sons and her husband" (Ruth 1: 3-5).

Naomi and her daughters-in-law, Orpah and Ruth, were now widows. At that time and in that culture, widowhood was a "distinct social class."[165] Women without a husband or father had no means of support. Women were not permitted to work outside the home or own property; they were, in fact, treated as property. Because of their lowly status women were "easily subject to falling victim to maltreatment from others."[166]

With the death of her husband and sons, Naomi had no choice but to return to her homeland of years before, Judah. There was no one in Moab to support her and she was forbidden from working. In Judah, she at least she had extended family.

Naomi's daughters-in-law, Orpah and Ruth, must have loved her very much because they wanted to go with her to Judah even though that would place them in jeopardy; they too were widows and they, unlike Naomi, had no family in Judah who could help them. Naomi urged them to remain in their home country: "*Go back, each of you to your mother's house. May the Lord deal kindly with you, as you have dealt with the dead and with me*" (Ruth 1:8). Weeping aloud and kissing her mother-in-law, Orpah remained in Moab (Ruth 1:4-14) but Ruth insisted on going with Naomi to Judah. In some of the most loving words of the Old Testament, Ruth proclaims to Naomi:

> "Where you go, I will go.
> Where you lodge, I will lodge.
> Your people shall be my people,
> And your god my God.
> Where you die, I will die —
> There will I be buried..."
> (Ruth 1:16-17).

Back in Judah, in the city of Bethlehem, Naomi and Ruth, like all widows, were dependent upon charity or family for survival. By custom, compassionate landowners would leave a portion of their crops on the outskirts of their fields for widows, orphans, and other poor in the community to gather. Ruth, stronger and younger than Naomi, went into the fields early every day to gather barley for herself and Naomi. By chance she went into the fields of Boaz, a distant relative of Elimelech.

One day, Boaz, walking by the field where Ruth was working, asked his servant who was in charge of the harvesters who the new gatherer was. The servant replied: "She is the Moabite who came back with Naomi from the country of Moab. She has been on her feet from early this morning until now, without resting even for a moment." Boaz approached Ruth, directed her where to gather the most barley, and invited her to drink from the vessels of his workers where, Boaz indicated, she could remain safe from young men who might molest her.[167] Ruth asked Boaz, *"Why have I found favor in your sight, that you should take notice of me, when I am a foreigner?"* (Ruth 2:10) Boaz answered, *"All that you have done for your mother-in-law since the death of your husband has been fully told me, and how you left your father and mother and your native land and came to a people that you did not know before. May the Lord reward you for your deeds, and may you have a full reward from the Lord, the God of Israel, under whose wings you have come for refuge"* (Ruth 2:11-12). In time, Boaz takes Ruth for his wife.

Ruth is one of only five women mentioned in the genealogy of Jesus (along with Tamar, Rahab, Bathsheba, the "wife of Uriah", and Mary.) (Matthew 1:5). That Ruth figures so prominently among all of the stories in the Old Testament and in the genealogy of Jesus, is significant theologically, culturally, and socially. As Joan Chittister notes, Ruth is "a Moabite, the lowest of the low, the woman without any status at all, out of whose line the greatest king of Israel shall come." In Chittister's words, "The point can hardly be any clearer: There is no one in whom God does not come to life. No one through whom God does not work."[168]

Ruth's and Naomi's ability to adapt is remarkable: through marriages, deaths of husbands, immigration to foreign lands, surviving in a difficult world, discovering — and rediscovering faith.

Behavioral Science On Adaptability

Essential to happiness and well-being is the ability to adapt to changing circumstances. In this sense, the skill of adaptability is inherent in other EQ skills, most notably, stress management and resilience. The ability to recognize when our circumstances have changed, accept our new reality, and pivot in light of it "is essential to enjoying a happy, satisfying life."[169] All of us "constantly meet psychological challenges but while some of us succumb, feel hopeless, disempowered, give up, others are able to meet challenges, take the knock and learn something from them." [170] Because life is full of changes, "our ability to have life satisfaction, to be happy, to have good relationships, depends on our ability to adapt."[171]

Adaptable individuals demonstrate the phases of adaptation: *courage* and *acceptance* of a new situation, and the ability to *pivot*.

- *Courage:* We often think of courage as charging into battle, running into burning buildings, or policing dangerous streets. But it takes just as much courage to face painful changes in life: the end of a marriage, alcoholism, the loss of a job, a terminal diagnosis, the death of a loved one, poor health. Having courage to realistically face unpleasant, frightening, or simply unexpected changes in our lives is essential if we are to effectively deal with life.[172]

- *Acceptance:* Accepting our changed circumstances involves not only acknowledging the reality of our new situation, but also accepting it: what can and cannot be changed; being able to abandon goals that are no longer feasible; intentionally redirecting efforts toward what can be changed. Acceptance is not the same thing as resignation; it is not giving up or quitting. Acceptance is realistic appraisal and active decision making." [173]

  Acceptance of our changed circumstances requires self-awareness and the humility to recognize what may be unpleasant truths: "My dream is unrealistic;" "My spouse no longer loves me," "My child has made some bad decisions," "The world is not as I thought." Only when we honestly face and accept our new reality can we begin to move forward to constructively cope with it.

  Notably, our "new direction" may be nothing apparent to the outside world. Rather, it may be a change within us, in how we perceive the world and our place in the world.

It is confidence, peace of mind, that comes with saying to ourselves, "Okay, I'm not as good as I thought at [abc], but I am good at [xyz], so I'll do [xyz]"; or, "Looks like my plans are not realistic, so I will make new plans"; or "Even though my spouse no longer loves me, I am a good person. I can move on"; or "Yes, my child has made some bad decisions, but I can still let her know I love her, set appropriate boundaries, and give her support for her to deal with the consequences of her actions."

- *Pivot:* Once we have faced our new situation and accepted it, we need to "reframe" it if we are to move forward. Pivoting requires creative flexibility, "reframing" as discussed in chapter three, and the imagination to see how our lives could be different.

    One morning, I spilled hundreds of dry cheerios in my reading chair and over dozens of books that sat on shelves next to my chair. I was furious. I was on a tight schedule and it would take forever to pick the cheerios out of the chair cushions, and from under and around all the books. And then, I thought of this chapter and what I had learned from it. I thought of the time I had been unable to get up from my chair during months of healing from foot surgery. I thought of friends who are bed-bound from illness. And I became grateful I could at least get up and pick all those darn cheerios. With that thought, nothing changed: the cheerios were still there until I picked them up. But everything changed. As my attitude and perspective, pivoted, I adapted to my new reality, took a breath, picked up the cheerios, and came out of the experience a better person, grateful in that moment for the health I too easily take for granted.

    The ability to pivot is a fundamental skill taught in cognitive therapy. [174] As Reverend Dr. John Claypool said, "We do not have the power to go back and undo or redo the past, but we do have the ability to 're-perceive' the past and decide what meaning we will assign to those events for the present and the future."[175]

We now turn to a modern-day hero, Andrea Edmonds, to see how she, like Naomi and Ruth, demonstrates courage, acceptance, and the ability to pivot when facing a challenge in her life.

Ruthie And Andrea
When Andrea Edmonds was pregnant with her third child, prenatal testing showed a marker for possible Down Syndrome. Because the

marker was also typical for normal babies, Andrea and her husband, Steve, did not pursue further testing. When their daughter, Ruthie, was born several months later, Andrea asked the nurse immediately after delivery if her daughter had Down Syndrome. The nurse said, "We have to do testing." Andrea could tell by the look on the nurse's face that Ruthie had Down Syndrome: "The one thing I feared more than anything before Ruthie was born was Down Syndrome but as soon as I held Ruthie, I knew. We can do this."

In the days after Ruthie's birth, friends and strangers reached out to Andrea and Steve. The director of RISE, a nationally acclaimed school for special needs children at the University of Alabama,[176] called Andrea with joyous "congratulations," providing information about the programs of RISE. Mothers and grandmothers of children born with Down Syndrome came to see Andrea with congratulations, information, and support. A friend from church whose son had mild cognitive impairment, wrote to Andrea, "As a parent, even before we have our children, we have all these plans for our children but what we learn is that we have to embrace God's plan for our children." The cards, notes, visits, calls, from these women meant the world to Andrea. They "shifted my mind set," Andrea said. "They taught me how to think. They showed me how to go about our life and be happy and be a family."

In the days and years ahead, whenever Andrea felt overwhelmed or had a tough question, she called one of these women, or would see them around town and ask them about whatever Ruthie questions were on her mind. They were always there for Andrea, and "so excellent in their encouragement," Andrea says, "in their endurance, in what they knew and shared." From these women, Andrea learned to resist trying "to plan out Ruthie's life as a whole," and instead, "to control what I could day by day, or moment to moment." Andrea learned, as she says: "Without a doubt we cannot figure out the ways of the Lord. Our Plan B may be God's Plan A. With each step we live out God's purpose."

As Ruthie grew older, her body shape began to change and it became harder to find clothing that fit her. Andrea was frustrated at the lack of cute, fashionable clothing available for Ruthie. Andrea had dressed her older daughter in beautiful clothes and wanted to do the same for Ruthie. Determined that Ruthie "deserved to look as precious as other children," Andrea searched everywhere for fashionable clothing. She could find nothing.

Andrea talked with her friend, Brian, whom she knew from exercise class, and with Silke, whom she knew from carpool line at Ruthie's school. Both Brian and Silke were faculty members at the University of Alabama in the Department of Clothing, Textiles, and Interior Design. Both designed clothing for clothing designers throughout the United States. [177] Andrea told them how hard it was to find clothes to fit Ruthie. Today, Brian and Silke design and make patterns and clothing for Ruthie. But not just Ruthie!

In 2010, determined that "all Down Syndrome girls deserve to look beautiful," and that "attractive clothing should be available to families who can't afford a Brian or a Silke," Andrea launched *Wonderfully Made*, an online and storefront clothing store that features beautiful clothing for Down Syndrome girls and others. Determined that such clothing should be available to those with limited means, part of Andrea's mission is to produce a clothing line at reasonable and affordable prices.

Andrea's online store features beautiful models, some of whom have Down Syndrome. All of the models are wearing cute, stylish clothes. A link on *Wonderfully Made*'s website tells of Ruthie's story and features joyful pictures of Ruthie and her friends playing. Everything about *Wonderfully Made* breathes its mission: "All girls are wonderfully made and are God's creation." Sunlight from full length windows fills *Wonderfully Made's* retail store. Colorful, beautiful dresses and blouses look like a garden in bloom. Jewelry designed for *Wonderfully Made* is displayed on the table behind a couch, along with books about Down Syndrome.

Andrea's priority when shoppers enter the *Wonderfully Made* online or retail or stores is that they feel "good and validated about themselves." She loves seeing little girls "cry when they come into the store because they have found something beautiful they can wear." She loves "seeing a woman or girl with a hard-to- fit size smile with joy when they come out of a fitting room and tell her, 'Thank you for valuing us to have these beautiful clothes in my size. Thank you for believing in me.'"

It was not an easy decision for Andrea to go into retailing. She had no background in retail, online marketing, or running a business. Establishing a career in clothing sales is not what she intended for her life. With an undergraduate degree in English and a Masters in English as a Second Language, Andrea is a teacher at heart: "I don't like to sell things and selling is not my strength." Launching *Wonderfully Made* was financially risky for Andrea and her family because when it opened, there was no apparent market for clothing for girls with Down Syndrome. Would it work? Was the world ready?

Faith guided Andrea through her hesitations and concerns. Throughout her life, Andrea's faith has grown as she faced and wrestled with doubt and questions. When she was in college Andrea called her parents "all the time" with questions about God. From them, she realized that "it's okay to have questions, that walking with the Lord is always questioning because faith doesn't always make sense, not in the way we think about other things." As Andrea says, her days of wrestling with her faith "opened my heart for those who would question how there could be a God who would create a child who as a disability. Why would He do that?" Her answer?

> *"The Lord's hand has become even more visible in my life as Ruthie gets older. I am more dependent on the Lord because I see how truly out of control life is. We cannot figure out the ways of the Lord. The human mind is not able to do that. But I've learned there is a purpose with each step we take. Whatever may happen, the Lord will give endurance, courage, to take the next step."*

And with that faith, Andrea opened *Wonderfully Made*, which now sells nationally and internationally.

The Ties That Bind Adaptability In Day-To-Day Life

Let us look at how the women of this chapter — Naomi, Ruth, Andrea — have demonstrated the courage, acceptance and the ability to pivot in the face of the challenges they have encountered. Naomi demonstrated adaptability throughout her life: as a young bride in Judah; as an immigrant to a new land; as a new mother, creating a new life in Moab; as a widow; as she buried one son, then the next; as she faced destitution and social ostracization; as she moved once again; as she struggled and regained her faith. Each time, Naomi adapted. In Moab, she developed strong and loving bonds with her daughters-in-law. She displayed courage, fortitude and decisiveness in moving back to Judah. She loved, supported, taught, and empowered Ruth. She was strong enough to question her faith, and willing to grow in her faith.

Naomi is the epitome of courage, acceptance of life, creative flexibility and undaunted love. In the words of Joan Chittister: "Naomi is a woman who knows how life works, and, powerless as she is in the system, she has great strength of self, great consciousness of her dignity... She knows herself to have a place in God's order of things."[178]

Ruth is a powerful role model of one who is able to adapt to major changes in life. Widowed as a young woman and left childless, she defied custom and culture by leaving her native land where her chances of starting a new life — meeting another husband, having children, being surrounded by extended family were excellent. Yet, devoted to Naomi, Ruth was willing to leave this security and opportunity to travel to a new land where she was a foreigner, an outcast marginalized by her race and her religion.[179] Once in Judah, Ruth continued to adapt to the challenges: she found work, worked hard, and used the resources available to her to support herself and Naomi.

Andrea epitomizes incredible adaptability, finding courage not just to accept the specialness of her daughter, but to see the opportunity in it to help Ruthie and thousands of others.

The stories of these women reveal lessons about emotional intelligence in general, beyond the skill of adaptability. Note the community they had around them. As noted in chapter eleven on strengths and weaknesses, community is important for any of us to be emotionally intelligent. Joan D. Chittister describes the relationship this community as *hesed*.[180] *Hesed* is a beautiful definition of community."[181] It is a Hebrew word that "describes a sense of love and loyalty that inspires merciful and compassionate behavior toward another person. Naomi and Ruth's *hesed* for each other grew to include people who consoled and befriended them when they moved to Judah (Ruth 1:12). Andrea's *hesed* included the strangers and friends who reached out to her after Ruthie's birth with information, congratulations, and joy, and Brian and Silke who turned Andrea's vision of clothing into reality. Andrea's *Wonderfully Made* clothing line creates *hesed* worldwide for girls and women.

The stories of this chapter show us that *hesed* is not limited by time or place. Ruth's *hesed* led to Jesus. Her son, Obed, became the father of Jesse, the father of David, ancestor of Jesus.[182] Andrea's *hesed* began years before Ruthie's birth when a football coach and his wife, Gene and Ruth Ann Stallings, the parents of Johnny, a boy with Down Syndrome, established RISE, the school where Ruthie attended. RISE is a preschool education program at the University of Alabama for specially made children — those with and without disabilities.

The stories of this chapter show faith permeating emotional intelligence. Note what Ruth said when Naomi urged her to remain in Moab, *"Your God will be my God"* (Ruth 1:15). Note how faith led Boaz to extend help to Ruth: *"May the Lord reward you for your deeds, and may you have a full reward from the Lord, the God of Israel, under whose wings you have come for refuge"* (Ruth 2:12). Note how her faith brought Andrea strength when Ruthie was born. When the delivery nurse placed her new baby in Andrea's arms, the following came to Andrea: *"Be joyful always, pray continually, give thanks in all circumstances."*[183] Andrea knew then that she could choose gratitude over despair.

Each of these women had to wrestle with their faith when they faced the challenges in their paths. Each was brave enough to honestly do so. As a result, they grew in their faith, which gave them strength for their journeys. Ruth had to turn away from the god of Moab[184] to embrace the God of Israel. When her life fell apart, Naomi became angry with God: *"the Almighty has dealt bitterly with me,"* (Ruth 1:19), but with the help of her friends, she returned to her faith with renewal: *"Blessed be the Lord"* for *"he is restorer of life and a nourisher of old age"* (Ruth 4:14). As Andrea says, "walking with the Lord is always questioning because faith doesn't always make sense, not in the way we think about other things." Through her searching for answers, Andrea found her faith becoming stronger, making the "Lord's hand even more visible" in her life, as she saw "how truly out of control life is," and learned that "there is a purpose with each step we live, that whatever may happen, the Lord will give endurance, courage, to take the next step."

Conclusion

One guarantee in life is that things will change. Whether we face these changes and adapt to them or let them overwhelm us, is our choice. The women of this chapter model for us emotional intelligence in how to adapt to the changes that can, and will, upend their lives; how to face our new situations courageously; how to accept our new reality; how to pivot inwardly and outwardly as we deal constructively with our changed circumstances.

Questions For Thought And Reflection

1. Have there been times when you've had to adapt to difficult changes? Looking back, did you go through the steps discussed in this chapter? Which step was most challenging?

2. The Book of Ruth is one of only three books in the Bible named for a woman and unique in that it focuses almost exclusively on women. As one commentator has written: "Throughout the story, women are at the center of the conversation, as speakers and as subjects; indeed, women are present in every scene of the story…. Women are portrayed as active and decisive, taking the initiative, able to set goals and achieve them."[185]

3. If the Bible was written today, what other women-centered stories would appear?

4. As we've noted, the Book of Ruth shows people supporting each other. It is also as Joan Chittister says, "a story of what it takes to discover the God within."[186] In your life, who are the people supporting you, and how have they helped you discover God within you?

5. Unlike much of the Old Testament, the Book of Ruth presents "no bloody battles, no immoral commands, no zealotry or hatred… It tells us nothing of purity or impurity, or prohibition or permission." "For what purpose then," asks Orit Avnery "was it written?" written?" Avnery suggests Ruth was written "to teach how great is the reward of those who do deeds of kindness." Do you agree? Is kindness the theme of Ruth? Or is it fortitude? Loyalty? What other themes do you see? Which theme is most relevant to you?

CHAPTER THIRTEEN: GRATITUDE

Of all of the emotional intelligence skills, gratitude is the most powerful antidote for negative emotions.[187] Learning to "bat the ball away" by focusing on gratitude when we find ourselves focusing on negative thoughts rewires the brain and thereby improves our physical and emotional wellbeing. This chapter looks at the story of Noah who built the ark and, in Cathy's words, her journey to joy through gratitude.

Noah

Imagine how you would feel if you were told that *"an end to all people"* was coming with *"floodwaters that cause every living thing on earth to perish: birds, livestock, wild animals, mankind."* (Genesis 6:5, 13, 17) Yet there is no record in scripture that Noah experienced fear upon hearing God's description of what was to come nor in God's command to Noah to build an ark and prepare for the oncoming apocalypse.

> *"Noah was a righteous man, blameless among the people of his time... Now the earth was corrupt in God's sight and was full of violence. God saw how corrupt the earth had become, for all the people on earth had corrupted their ways.*
>
> *"So God said to Noah, 'I am going to put an end to all people, for the earth is filled with violence because of them. I am surely going to destroy both them and the earth. Make yourself an ark...I am going to bring floodwaters on the earth to destroy all life under the heavens, every creature that has the breath of life in it. Everything on earth will perish. But I will establish my covenant with you, and you will enter the ark—you and your sons and your wife and your sons' wives with you.'*
>
> *"'You are to bring into the ark two of all living creatures, male and female, to keep them alive with you. Two of every kind of bird, of every kind of animal and of every kind of creature that moves along the ground will come to you to be kept alive. You are to take every kind of food that is to be eaten and store it away as food for you and for them...Seven days from now I will send rain on the earth for forty days and forty nights, and I will wipe from the face of the earth every living creature I have made.'*
>
> *"And Noah did all that the Lord commanded him. And after the seven days the floodwaters came on the earth. For*

> *forty days the flood kept coming on the earth, and as the waters increased, they lifted the ark high above the earth...Every living thing that moved on land perished—birds, livestock, wild animals, all the creatures that swarm over the earth, and all mankind.*
>
> *"But God remembered Noah and all the wild animals and the livestock that were with him in the ark, and he sent a wind over the earth, and the waters receded...By the twenty-seventh day of the second month the earth was completely dry.*
>
> *"So Noah came out [of the ark], together with his sons and his wife and his sons' wives. All the animals and all the creatures that move along the ground and all the birds—everything that moves on land—came out of the ark, one kind after another.*
>
> *"Then Noah built an altar to the Lord and, taking some of all the clean animals and clean birds, he sacrificed burnt offerings on it. The Lord smelled the pleasing aroma and said in his heart: 'Never again will I curse the ground because of humans, even though every inclination of the human heart is evil from childhood. And never again will I destroy all living creatures, as I have done.'" Genesis 6: 9-21*

How did Noah avoid being overwhelmed by fear when the floodwaters rose and rose, destroying "every living thing on the earth"? How did he find the strength to follow God's command to build the ark? How did he avoid the negative emotions that likely would blind and deafen the rest of us or at least cloud our senses? How did he overcome the fear that can grip the rest of us, clog our channel to Almighty God, block the Holy Spirit from free access to our spirit, turn us from our ability to be a channel of the Holy Spirit for others?

Noah's gratitude to Almighty God and total trust in the Lord gave him "eyes to see and ears to hear" God's word (Matthew 13: 16). Noah's obedience not only saved his family but also the entire human race. His emotional intelligence brought healing to the cosmos.

Behavioral Science On Gratitude

Behavioral science shows how gratitude in all forms is associated with happiness, pain management, improved sleep quality, managing stress, resilience, and less anxiety and depression.[188] It does so by rewiring our brains. When we are grateful, certain neural circuits are activated. In particular, our production of dopamine and serotonin increases. These hormones regulate our sense of happiness and wellbeing. Additionally, research studies show that when participants focus on things for which they are grateful, their brains show a marked reduction in the level of cortisol, a stress hormone. By reducing this stress hormone, gratitude significantly reduces symptoms of depression and anxiety.

Longitudinal studies of those who regularly engage in gratitude practices show that these individuals have better cardiac functioning and are more resilient to emotional setbacks and negative experiences.[189] Further studies have shown that receiving and displaying simple acts of kindness activates the hypothalamus which regulates sleep.[190]

At the neurochemical level, feelings of gratitude are associated with an increase in the modulation of the prefrontal cortex, the brain site responsible for managing negative emotions like guilt, shame, and violence. The more we focus on negative emotions, the more negative emotions we have. This is because our brain is conditioned to function in a repeated way. A person who worries too much about adverse outcomes will subconsciously rewire his brain to process negative information only. Our brains cannot focus on positive and negative information at the same time, thus by consciously practicing gratitude, we can train ourselves to selectively focus on positive emotions and thoughts, thus reducing anxiety and feelings of apprehension.[191] As Martin Seligman explains, "insufficient appreciation and savoring of good events in your past and overemphasis of the bad ones are the two culprits that undermine serenity, contentment, and satisfaction."[192]

Daniel Goleman presents study after study of the crucial role emotional intelligence plays not only in our ability to live healthy, complete lives but in our ability to bring healing and wholeness to others not only in our psychological health but even in our physical health. "Perturbing emotions are bad for health to a degree. People who experience chronic anxiety, long periods of sadness and pessimism, unremitting tension or incessant hostility, relentless cynicism or suspiciousness, were found to have *double* the risk of disease…distressing emotions [are] as toxic a risk factor as, say, smoking or high cholesterol are for heart disease."[193] He cites studies of the power of anger to damage the heart. And he quotes Yale researchers who point out "that it may not be anger alone that heightens the risk of death from heart disease, but rather intense negative emotionality of any kind that regularly sends surges of stress hormones through the body."[194] Yet Goleman asserts that "hostility is a habit that can be changed."[195] He quotes

Dr. Redford Williams of Duke University, "The antidote to hostility is to develop a more trusting heart. All it takes is the right motivation."[196]

Cathy

Gratitude for God's abundant blessings crashed into my life at the age of seventeen. I was struggling in prayer to comprehend how I could have been so blessed. While praying on a beautiful August day, I had an experience that in retrospect can only be described as "in the spirit." In reflecting on the abundance of blessings that had poured upon me especially that summer, I was overwhelmed at the immensity of God's goodness and how undeserving I was. While in the spirit, I realized that the only way I could respond to God was through gratitude and joy. The greatest joy I ever saw in my earthly father was when we were happy, especially when Mother would have us watch for him to come home from work every day and then let us race to the car, jumping into his arms in delight that he was home, or when we would open a Christmas or birthday gift from him and throw ourselves onto his lap, smothering him with kisses.

Although, on Earth, I could not treat my Heavenly Father in exactly the same way, scripture taught that I could still bring joy to my Heavenly Father but in a different way: by loving others as he had loved me. Frankly, this did not seem logical to me; it made no sense; I really could not understand how that could be a source of joy to him. Also, I could not comprehend how my giving to others could be anything other than a reduction in my gifts in this "zero-sum" world.

But frankly, at that moment, the immensity of my indebtedness for the abundance of his blessings was so great that it empowered me to try it. Gratitude forced me to my knees in surrender to him. Instead of focusing on me, a guarantee of misery, I decided to try focusing on the positive emotion of loving others and surrendering to God the negative emotions that were blocking me from joy.

As a teenager, it certainly was not "cool" to love others as Christ had loved us. Under any other circumstances, I never could have had the courage to smile at someone in the school hallway who did not smile at me. But on the next day, filled with the power of gratitude, I tried it, not for a reward for myself but just because it was the only way I could conjure to make God happy in response to the great happiness with which he had blessed me. I could love him in others. Focusing on him in them, I was empowered to feel love for them and to respond in love. To my absolute astonishment, I got a genuine smile in return from someone I did not know. Well, that just must have been a fluke, I thought, so I tried it again just to prove that it would not work. Lo and behold, I got another smile. Emboldened, I spent the rest of the day genuinely loving everyone I saw and have never felt so joyful at the end of a day in my life.

I committed to following Saint Paul's command to the Colossians, "Set your minds on things that are above, not on things that are on earth." (Colossians 3:2). If we will set our minds, concentrate at every moment on things that are above, on loving our Father above by loving his children as he has loved us, that habit of mind, powered by gratitude, will lead to joy *always*! Knowing that I deserved none of the blessings with which I had been showered, I lost all sense of entitlement in the overwhelming desire to express my gratitude for what I already had received.

Developing the habit of gratitude at a young age fueled a perpetual joy. I was truly living the passage in I Thessalonians: *"Be joyful always; pray continually; give thanks in all circumstances, for this is God's will for you in Christ Jesus."* Loving others was a continual prayer in a way, because with each act of love, no matter how small (and I definitely never did anything really big for anyone!), it felt as if I were saying to God, "Thank you;" in a sense, I was praying continually. That prayerful thankfulness in all circumstances had to have been God's will because it made me joyful always. He came that we might have life and have it abundantly.

Then, with each new day, the evidence grew that wanting nothing but His will resulted always in a better outcome than following what I wanted.[197] My capacity for decision-making on my own almost atrophied in the meantime. I just turned every decision over to him, knowing that his perfect will was the best thing I could possibly pray for or desire. And in every single case, it worked! Living in his will brought heaven here, brought the abundant life that Jesus said was God's will for us.[198]

Eventually, there was an existential threat to this system. I fell so deeply in love with Pettus Randall that, in the early years of our marriage, real fear of loss began to creep into my life. What would happen if he died before I did? I could not imagine life without him.

But death is inevitable. So I had a choice: I could live in fear of that eventuality for the rest of my life, insisting on having my own way and defying God's plan, or I could set my mind on things that are above, realizing that Pettus was a gift from above, not a possession of mine that I had earned. From that moment on, I gave thanks for the gift of each day that Pettus loved me and for the opportunity to love him back as Christ had loved me.

Shortly after his pancreatic cancer diagnosis on January 31, 2002, our minister asked me, "Cathy, what is your greatest concern as you face this with Pettus?" One answer came immediately to mind, but I waited even to articulate it, realizing what an important question it was and wanting to frame an answer that was genuine and true. I cannot possibly explain the comfort that overwhelmed me when I was able, after a full day of prayer and for every day thereafter, to confirm and articulate my very first thought: my greatest concern was truly that God's perfect will be done in our lives and he be glorified as we walked through the valley of the shadow of death. Because of my husband's faithful, courageous leadership, God was glorified on that walk.

In February 2002, Bishop Marc Andrus wrote in the monthly newsletter of the Episcopal Diocese of Alabama, "By being good, we are allowed to live the most deeply satisfying of lives as it is the life closest to the life of God. Not a life, you understand, without pain, but a life filled with joy." On its face, it seemed impossible to me that a life could be filled with joy in the face of pain, certainly the pain I was experiencing at that moment. Yet instantly, I realized that my life, although not without pain, was filled with joy. Genuinely, profoundly wanting his will over our own is the source of our greatest happiness, the source of our only true joy, the only way to be joyful always. As I walked with Pettus through the valley of the shadow of death, I truly feared no evil because we felt his presence and the strength and warmth of his loving arms upholding us every step of the way.

I had wondered if this way of living only worked in the good times, when I was feeling overwhelmed with gratitude for all the unmerited blessings in my life. But I found it to be true even in the deepest pain of loss: my life was filled with joy because with all of my heart, I wanted God's will and focused on loving him in others as he worked his purpose out. The journey through the valley of the shadow of death made a person of joy out of me even more than in the good times because it gave me the opportunity to prove to myself that death has no victory, the grave has no sting, we can give thanks in all circumstances, even at the edge of the grave. We can truly live into Philippians, 4:11-13: "I do not complain of want: for I have learned, in whatever state I am, to be content. I know how to be abased, and I know how to abound; in any and all circumstances, I have learned the secret of facing plenty and hunger, abundance and want. I can do all things in him who strengthens me." It is a matter of "setting our minds," as Colossians commands, of wanting his will above our own, of loving others, and being thankful in all circumstances.

Giving thanks always for everything as a gift made possible a life filled with joy even in the midst of pain.[199] Building my house on the solid rock of gratitude to God instead of on the sand of entitlement reaped the promises in Matthew 7:24-25.

Oswald Chambers says that the most practical thing imaginable is to love as God loves, that it is not something just sentimental or emotional. *This Christianity stuff worked*. The foundation held. I could live a live closest to life of God, not a life without pain, but a life filled with joy, even at the moment of greatest pain, the pain of losing Pettus.

The Ties That Bind Gratitude In Day-To-Day Life

Noah serves as one of the biblical examples of the importance of allowing total trust in God to drive out fear and the other negative emotions. As we have seen, negative emotions blind and deafen us or at least cloud our senses. They clog our channel, blocking the Holy Spirit from free access to our spirit and in turn from our abilities to be channels of the Holy Spirit for others. We don't have "eyes to see or ears to hear" (Matthew13:15-17) when we allow emotions such as fear, anxiety, anger, envy, etc. to take root in us.

The examples are legion in holy scripture of those who missed God's message because they were blinded or deafened in this way. Fear was the biggest cause, yet God's admonition to "fear not" appears 365 times in scripture, one for each day of the year. Even Moses and Paul, the shepherds and holy Mary, had to obey God's command to "fear not" before they could perceive and then obey.

Indeed, Saint Paul identifies the will of God for us: "Be joyful always; pray continually; give thanks in all circumstances for that is the will of the Father for you in Christ Jesus" (1 Thessalonians 5:16-18). We are commanded to process negative emotions as quickly as we are able so that our eyes that are blinded by fear, anger, anxiety, envy, etc. can be uncovered and we can know the joy of the Lord and can be a channel of that joy for others.

Had Noah been consumed with envy of his wealthier neighbors as they were eating and drinking and being merry, he would not have been able to hear the voice of God directing him to build the ark. Anger and fear at the debauchery that he saw in his world would have blinded him to the signs of God's purpose for his life. But Noah was a righteous man, the only righteous man, who stayed attuned to God through faith and hope and prayer. There was no cause for the negative emotions of guilt or shame because he was a man of righteous deeds. And the gratitude to God that he demonstrated by his first act after leaving the ark was the source of his power to keep anger, anxiety, and fear from disrupting the channel between him and his Lord.

Noah heard one voice. Noah found his way by following only one voice. We can safely assume that Noah's actions were challenged in that day. We can imagine the nay-sayers who doubted, those who criticized Noah's actions. It took courage and emotional intelligence for Noah to find gratitude and to keep finding gratitude daily as he acted on God's directions. Gratitude is not a one-time action. Some days it may be a minute-by-minute or hour-by-hour choice. But finding and living in gratitude is the key to our purpose and the key to our joy. May gratitude serve as the source of your joy and power all the days of your life.

Bat The Ball Away
Noah's example of focusing on only one voice, God's voice, inspired me to develop a gratitude habit of my own: In the decades since developing the habit of joy, I saw that whenever I let the "world" disrupt my surrender to my heavenly Father's will, I would lose focus. Negative emotions would flood back in and blind me to God's blessings. My gratitude would diminish, and then less gratitude led to less surrender which led to less focus: all resulting in less joy.

Through prayer, I discerned a solution. Realizing that I could think only one thought at a time, I decided to envision batting away negative thoughts the moment they emerge and replacing them with positive thoughts. Every time a negative thought arises, I hit it away as if I were playing tennis. It took time to develop this habit. First, I needed to locate the thought on my side of the court and analyze it. Negative thoughts have to be processed, or they will be repressed to emerge worse later. But by focusing and practicing this habit, I increased that processing speed to nanoseconds. As long as our minds and hearts contain negative emotions, there is no room for positive ones, for love.

Conclusion

There is a Zen fable retold by Benedictine Joan Chittister in her *Rule of Benedict: Insights for the Ages*.

A scholar by the name of Tokusan who was full of knowledge and opinions about the *dharma*, came to the Zen Master, Ryutan, and asked about Zen. Ryutan served tea to his guest. At one point Ryutan refilled his guest's teacup but did not stop pouring when the cup was full. Tea spilled out and ran over the table. "Stop! The cup is full!" said Tokusan. "Exactly," said Master Ryutan. "You are like this cup; you are full of ideas. You come and ask for teaching, but your cup is full; I can't put anything in. Before I can teach you, you'll have to empty your cup."[200]

Like Tokusan, we cannot fill our cups with gratitude if they are full of negative emotions. Gratitude has a long past in the history of ideas. Across cultures and time, experiences and expressions of gratitude have been treated as both basic and desirable aspects of human personality and social life.[201] Gratitude is a highly prized human disposition in Jewish, Christian, Muslim, Buddhist, and Hindu thought. And for good reason. Gratitude can help us free ourselves of negative emotions, empowering us to fill ourselves with positive emotions and live as we were meant to live: in God's image.

Questions For Thought And Reflection

1. Reflect on the story of Noah. Where do you see examples of Noah's gratitude? Are there places in your life where you can apply gratitude to overcome fear, anxiety, and other negative emotions?

2. Do you find that you focus more on positive emotions like gratitude or negative emotions like fear, envy, worry, etc? Does your focus change at different stages of life you experience? Why might that be?

3. Cathy uses a habit of thought from tennis to manage the inevitable influx of negative emotions that seek to find their way into her world. What habits might you develop?

4. A common reaction in humankind is to live negatively: the worry about the future, the need to succeed, the desire to have the most

excellent children. What promotes this negativity in our world? Is this an accurate worldview? How might this worldview mantra have invaded your thinking?

5. Noah's experience of living in an ark as he watched the world consumed and destroyed by floods had to be terrifying. Surely, he had to have wondered, Would the floods ever end? Would his family survive? Did they bring enough food? Can you look back on terrifying experiences in your life and with the benefit of hindsight, see them as leading you to a positive outcome that you never imagined to be possible when in the midst of your "floodwaters"?

6. What more would you like your faith to do for you?

CHAPTER FOURTEEN: CONCLUSION

It took almost a decade for this book to come to fruition. It began with a thirty second conversation of, "Do you want to write a book about emotional intelligence in the Bible?" "Sure, sounds fun," while loading dishes into a dishwasher. It evolved as we conceptualized, researched, collected stories, interviewed wise souls, obtained advice from readers, and wove it all together. During this process, life had a habit of interfering with our deadlines. What we thought would be a fairly straightforward process of pairing a biblical person and a modern-day person with an emotional intelligence skill was more complicated than we realized. But this longer-than-expected incubation period proved extraordinarily beneficial because it allowed us to expand the scope of this book, and to grow as people. As we were graced with the stories of those who shared their spiritual journeys with us, our understanding of emotional intelligence grew as did our reverence for the human spiritual longing.

We share in this chapter what we learned from the stories of this book, our aha moments. We saw that emotional intelligence is both more complicated and simpler than we thought; that our emotions are a gift from God that carry responsibility; that human connections, the bedrock of emotional intelligence, knows no boundaries of time, place, or culture; that heroes live among us; and that God's gift of emotions — and our capacity for emotional intelligence — is the way we can live lives of joy, contentment, and serenity, as well as the foundation for our spiritual growth. We invite you to consider whether these are your aha moments from this book, and also, what others?

Where Is "The List"?

One of our first aha moments came right away. We realized that emotional intelligence is both simpler and more complex than we had thought. Yes, there are basic principles that hold true for everyone. Emotional intelligence skills can help us in every aspect of our lives. Emotional intelligence is not something we are born with but is learned (or not) through life experience.

Different EQ skills help us in different ways. EQ skills are best understood and applied if we break them down into steps, as in, for example, we manage stress better if we use stress management skills (sense of control, purpose, and flexibility); we recover from setbacks, hardships, and adversities if we use resilience skills (realistic optimism, get a new perspective that comes from helping someone else, rely on faith); we cope better with life if we constructively manage the negative emotions that overwhelm all of us at times.

Beyond these basic principles, however, emotional intelligence can get confusing. Fast. There is, as you probably have realized throughout this book, an overlap between and among the various EQ skills. Stress management looks a lot like resilience, which looks a lot like adaptability, which looks a lot like gratitude and so on. We ran into this overlap problem from the beginning as we tried to organize chapters and coverage.

Naively at first, we thought the overlap would be fixed easily once we found the "master list" of EQ skills — something like the "Good Nutrition Pyramid," or the 5,000-mile Car Maintenance Guide, or the school supply list, but for EQ Skills. We assumed there would be a list that broke down emotional intelligence into discrete, usable, basic skills, definitions, and distinctions. Otherwise, emotional intelligence feels like mumbo jumbo, remaining conceptual not practical, amorphous not real, inaccessible not helpful in day-to-day life.

We also figured there would be a consensus among behavioral scientists on what this list is. To our dismay, we found there isn't. Throughout the rich trove of data sets, deeply researched academic articles, and the many books by behavioral scientists, there are multiple lists and many definitions and approaches. One expert identifies five basic EQ skills.[202] Another divides emotional intelligence into twenty-four "character strengths" and six groups.[203] Another set of experts identifies ten "traits."[204] The variations are endless, the terminology abundant, the emphases different. At that point, we realized that our first step for this book was to come up with a list of agreed-upon, basic EQ skills, definitions, and steps for implementation. The topics of chapters two through thirteen are the list we created.

Our relief at synthesizing a list of EQ skills with definitions, explanations, and steps for implementation was short-lived. This was our next aha moment and when we realized that while yes, of course, it is essential to appreciate the nuances of various EQ skills, it is also necessary to have a simple, bottom line on emotional intelligence. When life gets chaotic and emotions explode, which happens to all of us at least some of the time, we are incapable of thinking through a checklist of EQ skills. At that moment, we need something visceral, simple, powerful to grasp. And so here's our version of the bottom line on emotional intelligence: *1) Identify your emotion. No matter what the situation, stop, step back, figure out what you are feeling. 2) Think about what you can do about the situation and what you can't. 3) Be grateful for what you have in that moment.* If we can follow these three steps when we encounter hurdles in life, we can be in control of our emotions rather than being hijacked by them, and that is emotional intelligence. In our opinion and that of most behavioral scientists, the last step is especially important. Focusing on what we can be grateful for, even in the midst of despair or terror, orients our perspective from hopelessness to hope.

Now that we had our list of EQ skills and simple summary of them, we still had to wrestle with the fact that no matter how we organized emotional intelligence, there is overlap among the EQ skills. We confronted this fact repeatedly as we tried to figure out whom to profile in which chapter.

Moses, for example, would fit beautifully in the chapter on resilience or in the chapter on stress management, but we put him in the chapter on self-awareness. We did so because of what we learned about self-awareness from Moses. We saw how Moses grew into self-awareness, from an impulsive young man unable to control his rage to a person of maturity and wisdom who became able to see what many of us can never see, the burning bush in our lives. Moses, the heroic figure of children's Bible stories, was in fact, like us all, a flawed human being. His life teaches a fundamental lesson not only about self-awareness but also about emotional intelligence in general: emotional intelligence is not a trait we are born with but wisdom we have the opportunity to gain through life experience.

Once we began to see this deeper truth about self-awareness, we knew we had to put Betty Shirley's story into the self-awareness chapter with Moses because Betty Shirley, like Moses, shows how self-awareness grows in the valleys of life. If it was hard for Moses to confront the Pharaoh and lead a bunch of unruly, ungrateful, impatient Hebrews in a desert for forty years, Betty's feat was difficult in another, interior way. She had to find the courage to face not only that she had depression, but to do so at a time in the United States and in a small, rural town in the deep south, when mental illness carried stigma and scorn. Yet Betty, supported by her loving family, bravely faced her mental illness which allowed her to seek help, to heal, and like Moses, to lead others lost in the wilderness.

And so it went. Peter fit into the chapter on emotional stability not only because he epitomized emotional stability but because he had to work so hard at it. Peter had to harness his explosive, mercurial personality, and that was not easy. But Peter grew through his tribulations and trials, beyond his betrayal of his friend, beyond his impulsivity into emotional stability. As Peter's journey shows, an emotional intelligence skill that is hard-won is all the more powerful because it is hard-won. When Peter was able to stabilize his large personality, what had been explosiveness became strength, giving Peter the laser focus he needed to carry on Jesus's teachings.

Alyce would have fit in any number of chapters because her life exemplifies so many EQ skills, but we put her with Peter in the emotional stability chapter because of what she taught us about the fuel needed for emotional stability. Alyce's deep gratitude for everything in her life helped her get through not only the dark times of her mother's alcoholism but to grow from that experience, to thrive, and to become, like Peter, a strong and inspiring leader. Alyce personifies the bottom line of emotional intelligence: gratitude is the foundation for every EQ skill.

As we moved people from chapter to chapter trying to figure out where they fit best, finally landing them in a spot, we grew to appreciate that EQ skills, precisely because they overlap, make for a more effective team. When the players on a team are each in their own right a strong player, the team is stronger. When a player on such a team is having a bad day, the team is still strong because the other players can take up the slack. So it is for us. If our EQ skill of, for example, self-awareness, emotional stability, or managing negative emotions is "having a bad day," our other EQ skills can cover and allow the "injured player" to heal and rebuild.

In these ways, those things that confounded us at first in organizing this book: the lack of a "master list"; the need to delineate and explain; the just-as-strong need to simplify; what to do about the overlap of EQ skills — are what helped us see what we could not see before. We saw how emotional intelligence is not what we are born with but what we all have the opportunity to grow into. We saw that the most fertile soil for such growth is when we are brought to our knees by life. Through the stories of those who shared some of their lives with us, we learned to cherish the overlap of EQ skills because the overlap is what makes us strong.

Resources And Gifts

Liz's comments about resources in Chapter Four on tesilience and Barry's comments about "doing our part" in chapter six on habits, blended together beautifully as we worked on this book. Liz overcame overwhelming odds in her young life. In the depths of despair, she saw God at work in her life, making resources available to help her cope with the hard times. For Liz, these resources were her teachers. As Liz said, "I learned that even if a person is born into terrible circumstances like I was, God can provide the resources needed for success." Barry, Pam's wise neighbor, told us when we were talking with him about the habits in life: "God has always provided for all of my needs, even in the midst of unfathomable grief. He was there for me. But I am expected to do my part." Together, Liz' and Barry's words became one of the themes of this book: emotions are a resource God gives us, but we must do our part to manage them wisely.

As shown throughout the stories of this book, emotions become a resource for us because they provide important information. Positive emotions like joy, happiness, and contentment tell us that whatever we are doing, or whomever we are with, are good for us. Negative emotions also guide us. Fear warns us of danger. Sadness saps our energy, keeping us still, protecting us, in a way, so we do not venture forth when we are unable to make wise decisions. Anxiety tells us we need to manage our stress better. Shame may be telling us we have not lived up to the values we hold.

In this sense, emotions are a gift, given to us by God because regardless of whether we are experiencing positive or negative emotions, the information they provide gives us the opportunity to grow in wisdom. But to grow, we need to do our part, to assess: What is the information my emotions are providing? How do I use this information appropriately? When have my emotions outlived their usefulness? What changes do I need to make? As Barry says, using the skills of emotional intelligence to address these questions is how we do our part with the gift of emotions God has given to us.

We are free to see our emotions as a gift and grow in our ability to manage them, or not. Freedom, like emotions, is also a gift from God. We are free to use emotional intelligence or not. Some days it is hard to be emotionally intelligent. We are all masters at convincing ourselves that the things, substances, acquisitions, achievements for which we lust are the salve we need to fill our emptiness. Solomon began his reign as a wise and humble king but lost his way in the trappings of grandeur and wealth. David, Solomon's father, lost his way by ordering the murder of an innocent man to get what he wanted: the man's wife. Tammy, Nick, and Alyce's mother sought refuge in drugs and alcohol, hurting themselves and all of those who loved them. Emotional intelligence is how we can learn to resist the unhealthy urges that at times plague us all.

Throughout the stories of this book, we see examples of people who chose to learn from their emotions and make constructive changes based on the information they provide. Both Bryan Stevenson and John Dorsey paid attention to the dissatisfaction they felt with the career paths they were on: Bryan, who was headed toward a traditional law practice and John, who was in a traditional psychiatric practice. Both redirected their careers in ways that were more fulfilling to them. Ray Hinton, self-aware enough to see that his anger was killing him, prayed to God to help him forgive those for whom he had hatred in his heart. Only then, Ray realized, would he be free and able to feel, once again, the joy he had once felt. Nick and his family learned to move beyond shame to become national leaders for Campus Recovery Centers on college campuses throughout the United States.

In this way, Liz and Barry gave us all an *aha* moment: that emotions are a gift given to us by God to navigate life, and emotional intelligence is how we "do our part" with this gift.

Connections And Community
One of the basic principles of emotional intelligence is that being connected to other people is important to being emotionally intelligent. We saw this come to life as we put this book together. Social connections occur most obviously and most often with those we live with and among, but as the stories of this book show, powerful social connections also can arise with those with whom we share a fleeting moment, those who lived thousands of years ago, or even those with whom we seemingly share only differences.

The power and strength of connections with those in our midst is shown in the support of Alyce's father, brother, and church members who held her up as her mother disappeared into alcoholism; in the women who surrounded Andrea after the birth of her daughter, Ruthie, born with Down Syndrome; in the friends who saved Paul's life by sneaking him out of town in the dark of the night; in the women who comforted Naomi and Ruth when they arrived as refugees in Bethlehem from Moab.

The depth of social connections with those we do not know, or barely know, but who can profoundly impact us in a momentary encounter include Henry Hill, the prisoner on Alabama's death row who met Bryan Stevenson when Bryan was a law student.

Their encounter helped Bryan find purpose in his practice of law. The people Jesus met for a moment: the paraplegic, the woman being stoned, the man who lived among the tombs, were forever changed by their brief encounters with Jesus. Demarcus, as a five-year-old in an Atlanta hospital battling kidney cancer, was changed profoundly by the dozens of health care professionals who took care of him.

Pairing a biblical person with a modern-day person brings home the truth that our connection to other human beings knows no time, place, or cultural limits. As a young girl, Liz found comfort in the story of Joseph from thousands of years ago. Bryan found solace in Paul's guidance about the brokenness in all of us. Demarcus found strength in the spirituals sung by slaves from over a hundred years ago. Moses as a young man knew the fire of uncontrollable anger, just like us. The woman being stoned by the crowd for adultery felt the pain of shame, just like us. Joseph felt the crushing weight of one set back after another, just like us. Everyone, whether they lived thousands of years ago or today on the other side of the world or on the opposite end of the political spectrum, loses loved ones and grieves; feels terror over poor decisions made by their children — or by ourselves; are bowed by the unfairness of life. That there can be a bond across time, place, and culture demonstrates the universality of human nature in a fractured world in which human beings are joined together by the anguishes, and joys, of life.

Ordinary Heroes

When we began this project, we thought about profiling famous individuals as modern-day examples of emotional intelligence. But as soon as we started collecting stories, we realized that there were plenty of individuals in our daily lives to fill hundreds of chapters. It has been a joy to reach out to some of these remarkable individuals and invite them to tell us their stories.

It's also been fun to reflect on how we were led to them. Our friend, Pam Parker, told us about Demarcus whom she had recently met in the student union building at the University of Alabama, empty because of covid lockdowns. Demarcus, the student body president, was the only person in the building the day Pam went to talk about a community reading program she was starting. Our friends at the University of Alabama's Campus Recovery Center led us to Tammy. Our friend, Gina, excited about meeting the founder of a new clothing store in town, led us to Andrea, Ruthie, and *Wonderfully Made*. Liz was a law student of Pam's and serves on community boards with Cathy. Betty Shirley has been a friend for years through church and community events; Bryan Stevenson since moving to Alabama in the 1980's; Alyce through friends, community, and work. And so it went. Each person we profiled was right in front of us. We invite you to consider if this might be true for you. Who do you know who shows remarkable emotional intelligence in facing their adversities in life?

Ripple Effects
We have been struck by the ripple effects of chance meetings in the stories we have collected. Meeting Henry Hill helped inspire Bryan to found the *Equal Justice Initiative* which has impacted hundreds of individuals condemned to die, to EJI's founding of *The Legacy Museum* which attracts 400,000 visitors each year,[205] to Bryan writing *Just Mercy*, which became a New York Times bestseller and major motion picture teaching millions of people about the injustices of the American justice system.

Bill Wilson, a stockbroker during the 1929 crash of the American stock market, sought to maintain his sobriety by helping Bob Smith, another alcoholic. They founded Alcoholics Anonymous, an international fellowship with over two million members. Almost one hundred years later, Tammy attended an AA meeting and decided to turn her life around.

Ray Hinton, a black man, befriended Henry Hays, a white supremacist in a neighboring cell who was sentenced to death for beating and lynching a black teenager. Friendship with Henry helped Ray forgive those who had wrongly convicted him.

The ripple effects of these stories and others in this book helped us see how the mystery and power of human connections knows no limits. We close in prayer.

Dear God,
Wrap your loving arms around us as we come together. We do not know fully who or what you are,
But we know we have seen you,
In the vulnerability of the woman who was stoned,
The courage of Nick and his family,
The self-awareness of Moses and Betty Shirley,
The resilience of Joseph and Liz,
The emotional stability of Peter and Alyce,
The wisdom Barry shared with Pam and Cathy,
The battles waged by David and Tammy,
And by all of us, one way or another.

We have seen you in the perseverance of Paul and Bryan,
The forgiveness of Ray,
The empathy of John,
The strength of Job and Demarcus,
The embrace of change by Naomi, Ruth, and Andrea, and
The gratitude of Noah.

Thank you for sending us emotions of
sadness, anxiety, grief,
Angels who disturb the waters of our souls,
To guide us,
To stop us,
To get us to pay attention, To help us be still,
To care for ourselves,
To make changes.

Thank you for sending us
Emotions of joy, happiness and lovingkindness,
Angels who teach our souls to sing
And empower us to love others as you have loved us.

*Thank you for those who have gone before us
And those who go beside us,
Who show us that we are not alone,
That we can do it too,
Because we are creatures made in your image.*

Amen.

Questions For Thought And Reflection

1. Thinking back through this study:
   - Which biblical person resonates with you? Why?
   - Which modern day person resonates with you? Why?
   - Which EQ skill resonates with you? Why?

2. Recall the assessment you did of your EQ skills at the beginning of this study. Reassess, using the Table of Contents as your list of skills and the same assessment scale: "1" for "use this a lot," "2" for "use this some of the time," and "3" for "could use improvement." Compare your assessment at the beginning of this study. Any changes?

3. Looking back over your life, can you see times when your emotional intelligence grew? Was it in the "valleys" of life? How so?

4. What information are your emotions currently providing to you? Are you allowing any of your emotions to outlive their usefulness? What can you do "to do your part" and use wisely the information your emotions are providing to you?

5. Think through the communities that have embraced and surrounded you:
   - Who are those who live among you who have helped you along the way of life?
   - Who are those with whom you have had a brief, momentary contact but who profoundly impacted you?
   - Have you found community and connection with those who lived many years ago? With whom and how did it happen?

- Have you, or can you, find community with those with whom you seemingly share only differences? What might that look like?

- When have you been the social connection another person needed?

6. We've given our "bottom line" of emotional intelligence: *Identify your emotions. No matter what the situation, stop, step back, figure out what you are feeling. Think about what you can do about the situation and what you cannot. Be grateful for what you have in the moment."* Does this speak to you? If not, what would you change so that it does?

7. What more would you like your faith to do for you? How might you use EQ skills to grow in your faith?

APPENDIX A: LECTIO DIVINA AS A MEDITATION PRACTICE FOR THE LESSONS OF THIS BOOK

Lectio Divina is an ancient practice of reading, meditation, prayer, and contemplation. "The phrase *lectio divina* means 'divine reading' in Latin. It is a prayer practice for "listening to Scripture with the ear of the heart, for entering into a **"a dialogue with God through scripture** that includes the whole self: thoughts, images, memories, desires." The prayer practice of lectio divina arose in the sixth century monastic communities in the sixth century as a way of communicating with God through scripture. *

We invite you to use *Lectio Divina* to meditate, pray, and contemplate the Bible passage in each chapter. Use *Lectio Divina* for some or all of the chapters, as you choose. *Lectio Divina* is a powerful and mystical experience whether done alone or with a group. Use *Lectio Divina* to explore how the people of the chapter(s) you have chosen used emotional intelligence to face life challenges. Contemplate how that person's emotions were a gift from God. Consider how that emotion is a gift from God in your life, and what emotional intelligence skills you can bring to honor this gift.

Begin *Lectio Divina* by sitting comfortably, placing both feet on the ground, with posture upright and hands open on your lap as if waiting to receive a gift from God. Then abandon any agenda, worries, or thoughts you bring to this prayer and entrust these things to the providence of God. Ask for the grace to be receptive to what God will speak to you through this scripture reading.

READ (lectio)
Choose a portion of the scripture passage in the chapter you have a chapter that speaks to you and which tells you something about the Biblical person highlighted in that chapter. Slowly and meditatively read aloud that passage. Listen for a particular word or phrase that speaks to you and sit with it for a time.

MEDITATE (meditatio)

Read the same passage a second time. As you re-engage the text, focus on how the biblical character used or struggled to use the particular emotional intelligence skill of the chapter. Let that biblical person's journey be your invitation to dialogue with God about your journey in life.

PRAY (oratio)

Read the text a third time. Allow the words to wash over you and permeate your thoughts and feelings as you consider what God is saying to you with this story. What do you want to say to God? What feelings does this story raise up in you? Share your answers with God.

CONTEMPLATE (contemplatio)

Read the text one final time. As you do, release the word or phrase you have been praying with. Be still and rest in God's embrace. What gift has God given you to take away from this practice of *Lectio Divina*? To what action might God be inviting you? How can you employ the emotional intelligence skill in your life? Thank God for this gift and invitation as you conclude your prayer.

*Quotations are from: https://mcgrathblog.nd.edu/how-to-practice-lectio-divina-praying-with-scripture

APPENDIX B: MINDFULNESS MEDITATION

Appendix A offers one type of meditative practice, *Lectio Divina*, which invites you to think about and analyze a biblical passage to support you in acting upon the word of God in your daily life. This Appendix (B) offers tips on how to meditate in another way.

How To Practice Meditation

Meditation may be done in private or with others. You may use a video (or app) to offer guidance, listen to music, or practice in silence. Be open to trying different styles (such as loving- kindness or mantra), lengths of time, and locations until you find what feels right for you.

- Set aside time: Start with two minutes, maybe five, knowing that your commitment can grow into longer meditations. Research suggests ten to twelve minutes of meditation is where the most benefits are gained.

- Designate a space: Where are you most comfortable? You could meditate outside, inside, even at work. Try to find a location where there are minimal distractions, noting that ambient sounds (wind, birds chirping, and the like) may benefit your practice.

- Set yourself up for success: Turn off your phone ringer and set a timer. If using a guided meditation, you can trust the guide will stop you. If practicing alone, setting a timer can help you avoid wondering, "Am I done yet?"

- Make meditation a habit: Meditation is a *practice*. Commit to trying daily, even if you don't get through the full time, even if you feel your mind and focus are wandering— committing to the practice is helpful for establishing the routine. And trying different places, times, etc. is part of that practice! What you need for comfort may change.

- Being mindful

- Here are some steps to settling into a mindfulness meditation:

- Set your timer.

- Decide on body position: You know your body best, so find comfort before you begin the meditation.
    - Sit in a chair with both feet on the floor.
    - Sit on the floor with crossed legs (lotus). Consider putting a blanket under your hips for comfort.
    - Lay down (*savasana*), with support under your knees and head/neck.
- Close your eyes.
- Set an intention. This can be a goal. It can be a wish. Examples:
    - I am happy.
    - I am confident.
    - I am loved.
- Take a few slow, deep breaths, in and out through your nose. If helpful, count as you do this (e.g., 3 count in, 3 count out). Breathe in the air that gives you life. Breathe out everything that does not serve your intention. Out goes stress, fear, the grocery list … anything that is not specific to your present mindful moment.
- Meditate. As you practice, take note of what you think or feel, and let it go—like you're in a museum, look at what's there and leave it as you move along. Thoughts and feelings will come up, note them, see them, and then without judgment, let go. You can always return to counting breaths as a way to ground yourself. Some other examples:
    - Finger breathing. Trace the contour of one hand with the other. Inhale as you go up each finger, exhale as you go down. Repeat, switching hands, slowing the pace, whatever feels comfortable.
    - Body scan. Start at the top of your head and shift your focus down your body. Take a few extra breaths in areas that feel tense or pain or are tied to emotions. Breath into those spaces, breathe out what isn't useful for them. Another option is to imagine a light shining into each part of your body as you scan it.

- Guided meditations may take you for a virtual walk in the woods or along the beach. They may take you to different points in your life. And they offer different levels of instruction. If choosing a guided practice, find a voice, tone, and pace that works for you.

ENDNOTES

1. Jon Kabat-Zinn, Full Catastrophe Living 287 (Delta Books 1990).

2. https://www.youtube.com/watch?v=QX_oy9614HQ.

3. Thomas Merton, Merton's Life and Writings, *quoting* Meister Eckert, a thirteenth-century German theologian.

4. *Cf.* Sue Monk Kidd, First Light 14 (Penguin Books 2006).

5. Daniel Goleman, Emotional Intelligence: Why It Can Matter More Than IQ 172 (New York: Bloomsbury, 1995).

6. *Ibid* at 177.

7. Acts 8:1, 9:1; BRUCE Chilton, Rabbi Paul: An Intellectual Biography (Image Books, Doubleday 2004).

8. Southwick & Charney, Resilience 165-183 (Cambridge University Press 2012).

9. Robert M. Sapolsky, Why Zebras Don't Get Ulcers, 22 — 50 Hold Paperbacks 2004).

10. Medina, Brain Rules 173 (Pear Press 2008); Robert M. Sapolsky, Why Zebras Don't Get Ulcers, at 37-50; HANS Selye, The Stress of Life 97-127 (McGraw-Hill 1976); *Stress Weakens the Immune System*, Am. Pyschol. Ass'n (Feb. 23, 2006) http://www.apa.org/research/action/immune.aspx; (2006); *How Your Brain Responds to Stress*, The Franklin Institute, http://www.fi.edu/learn/brain/stress.html.

11. Medina, Brain Rules at 176-188.

12. Selye, The Stress of Life at 218-246 (discussing inflammatory diseases, focal infections, arthritis, and rheumatic and rheumatoid diseases caused or exacerbated by stress).

13. Sapolsky, Why Zebras Don't Get Ulcers at 81 (In a stress response, if food and water are already in your large intestine, "everything

gets pushed through too fast for the water to be absorbed optimally. Diarrhea, simple as that.").

14. Medina, Brain Rules at 176-188.; *cf.* Selye, The Stress of Life at 203-212 (discussing the hypertension that results from a "transient corticoid overdosage").

15. *Ibid* at 177-78; *cf.* Sapolsky, Why Zebras Don't Get Ulcers at 202-225.

16. Medina, Brain Rules at 178.

17. David Watson, *Positive Affectivity*, Handbook of Positive Psychology 207-16 (Oxford University Press 2009).

18. Pamela Bucy Pierson, Ashley Hamilton, Michael Pepper, Megan Root, *Stress Hardiness and Lawyers*, 42 Journal of the Legal Profession 1 *(2018)*.

19. Viktor E. Frankl, Man's Search for Meaning (Beacon Press 2006).

20. Laura A. King, Joshua A. Hicks, Jennifer L. Krull & Amber K. Del Gaiso, *Positive Affect and the Experiences of Meaning in Life*, 90 J. of Personality and Social Psychology 179 (2006).

21. Bryan Stevenson, Just MERCY (Spiegel & Grau 2015).

22. *Ibid* at 38-41.

23. 23. Ibid at 67, 250, 68.

24. 24. Ibid at 204.

25. John Grisham, https://www.goodreads.com/review/show/1080847201

26. Keith Schneider, *Revitalizing Montgomery as It Embraces Its Past*, NY Times, May 21, 2019; https://museumandmemorial.eji.org/museum.

27. Bryan also has an outlet that gives him a respite from stress. He plays the piano. Bryan is a concert pianist, even playing at the Lincoln Center with Winton Marseilles in a fundraiser

for EJI. *Freedom, Justice and Hope,* https://www.youtube.com/watch?v=6VO9iYds9ag&ab_channel=JazzatLincolnCenter).

28. Bryan Stevenson, Just Mercy at 285-287.

29. 2 Corinthians 12:8.

30. Bryan Stevenson, Just Mercy at 287.

31. Bryan Stevenson, Just Mercy at 11, 10-13.

32. Peter Hauri & Shirley Linde, No More Sleepless Nights 106 (John Wiley & Sons 1991); *see also* Selye, The Stress of Life *supra* note 20, at 173-178 (self- observable signs of stress).

33. Daniel Goleman, *Emotional Intelligence* 177 (Bantam Books 1995).

34. Frederick Buechner, Wishful Thinking 2 (Harper One 1993); Jamie S. Hughes, Mary K. Gourley, Laura Madson, & Katya LeBlanc, *Stress and Coping Activity: Reprograming Negative thoughts,* Teaching of Psychology 38(1) 36-39 (2011) "Individuals afflicted with depression and anxiety are often overwhelmed with all-or-none and negative thinking. They have difficulties thinking positively and generating thoughts that can help them cope with their situation."

35. Martin Seligman, *Authentic Happiness 35, 36* (Free Press 2002).

36. *See also* Daniel Goleman, *Emotional Intelligence 177* (Bantam Books 1995); Pamela Bucy Pierson, *The Business of Being a Lawyer 41, 50* (West Academic 2014).

37. *Ibid* at 36.

38. *Ibid* at 35.

39. *Ibid*

40. *Ibid*

41. Jamie S. Hughes, Mary K. Gourley, Laura Madson, & Katya LeBlanc, *Stress and Coping Activity: Reprograming Negative thoughts,* Teaching of Psychology 38(1) 36-39 (2011) "Individuals afflicted with depression and anxiety are often overwhelmed with all-or-

none and negative thinking. They have difficulties thinking positively and generating thoughts that can help them cope with their situation."

42. The Psychology of Purpose, John Templeton Foundation 10 (2018) https://www.templeton.org/wp-content/uploads/2020/02/Psychology-of-Purpose.pdf; Harlow, L.L. Newcomb, M.D. & MeBentler, P.M. *Depression, Self-derogation, Substance Use, and Suicide Ideation: Lack of Purpose in life as Mediational Fact,* Journal of Clinical Psychology 42, 5-21 (1986); Martin Seligman, Authentic Happiness 260, 250-263 (Free Press 2002).

43. The Psychology of Purpose, John Templeton Foundation 10 (2018) https://www.templeton.org/wp-content/uploads/2020/02/Psychology-of-Purpose.pdf

44. The Psychology of Purpose, John Templeton Foundation 10 (2018) https://www.templeton.org/wp-content/uploads/2020/02/Psychology-of-Purpose.pdf

45. In 2021, Kathy and Ray Hayes were given the Collegiate Recovery Philanthropist of the Year Award, given annually by the Association of Recovery in Higher Education, the award recognizes those who have made extraordinary and significant contributions to collegiate recovery.

46. Daniel Goleman, *Emotional Intelligence 214* (Bantam Books 1995).

47. Mark Twain, *The Adventures of Tom Sawyer* (Sea Wolf Press 2018).

48. James Swanson, *Dictionary of Biblical Languages With Semantic Domains: Hebrew (Old Testament)* (Electronic ed. Oak Harbor: Logos Research Systems, Inc., 1997).

49. Steven M. Southwick, M.D. and Dennis S. Charney, M.D., *Resilience: The Science of Mastering Life's Greatest Challenges 7* (Cambridge University Press 2015).

50. *Ibid*

51. *Ibid* at 29.

52. *Ibid*

53. *Ibid*

54. *Ibid* at 24.

55. Wayne Muller, *A Life of Being, Having, and Doing Enough* 187-189 (Three Rivers Press 2010).

56. *Ibid* at 81.

57. *Ibid*

58. *Ibid* at 85.

59. *Ibid* at 88.

60. *Ibid* at 92.

61. *Ibid*

62. *Ibid*

63. *Ibid*

64. Elizabeth Huntley, *More Than a Bird* (Salt House Publishing 2015).

65. Steven M. Southwick, M.D. and Dennis S. Charney, M.D., *Resilience: The Science of Mastering Life's Greatest Challenges* (Cambridge University Press 2015). Southwick and Charney's book is an excellent, highly readable, enjoyable and informative resource on resilience.

66. *Ibid* at 25, 29.

67. *Ibid* at 52.

68. *Ibid* at 53.

69. *Ibid*

70. *Ibid*

71. *Ibid* at 58-62.

72. *Ibid* at 66.

73. *Ibid* at 81.

74. Steven M. Southwick, M.D. and Dennis S. Charney, M.D., *Resilience: The Science of Mastering Life's Greatest Challenges 81-99* (Cambridge University Press 2015).

75. *Ibid* at 100.

76. *Ibid* at 115.

77. *Ibid*

78. *Ibid* at 128-142.

79. *Ibid* at portions of 143.

80. *Ibid* at 165; 165-183.

81. *Ibid* at 185

82. *Ibid*

83. *Ibid*

84. Daniel Goleman, *Emotional Intelligence 215* (Bantam Books 1995).

85. *Ibid*

86. *Ibid* at 217.

87. *Ibid* at 221.

88. See Chapter Two.

89. See Chapter Seven.

90. Daniel Goleman, Emotional Intelligence 227

91. *Ibid* at 226.

92. *Ibid* at 226.

93. *Ibid* at 225

94. E.H. Plumptre, *Bible Educator*, Vol. IV at 129 (Nabu Press 2011).

95. Charles Duhigg, *The Power of Habit: Why We Do What we Do in Life and Business 25* (Random House 2012).

96. 1 Kings 1, 28-30; 2:1-2;3:5-14. The story of Solomon can be found in 1 Samuel, 1 Kings and 1 Chronicles.

97. Pamela Pierson, *The Business of Being a Lawyer 5* (West Academic 2014).

98. Charles Duhigg, *The Power of Habit 15* (Random House 2012).

99. Emotional Regulation, Yale Center for Emotional Intelligence, ei.yale.edu

100. c. 1009/1001-969 B.C.E.

101. (https://www.myjewishlearning.com/article/king-david/)

102. Daniel Goleman, Emotional INTELLIGENCE xiv (London Bloomsbury 1995).

103. M. M. Kobiruzzaman, https://newsmoor.com/emotional-intelligence- eq-importance-characteristics-how-to-improve/#:~:text=Five%20 Characteristics%20of%20Emotional%20Intelligence%20%28EQ%29%201%20 Self-Awareness.,...%204%20Empathy.%20...%205%20Social%20Skills.%20, September 20, 2020.

104. *Ibid*

105. Alcoholics Anonymous by Alcoholics Anonymous 53 (Alcoholic Anonymous World Service, Inc 4th Ed.2002).

106. Wikipedia viewed on Aug.26,2021.

107. Daniel Goleman, Emotional Intelligence at 43, 47 (Bantam Books 1995).

108. John D. Mayer and Alexander Stevens, *An Emerging Understanding of the Reflective (Meta) Experience of Mood*, unpublished manuscript (1993), https://ohsu.pure.elsevier.com/en/publications

109. Goleman identifies self-aware, engulfed and accepting as the three styles of attending to and dealing with emotions. Daniel Goleman, Emotional Intelligence at 48 (Bantam Books 1995).

110. Daniel Goleman, Emotional Intelligence at 43, 47 (Bantam Books 1995); John D. Mayer and Alexander Stevens, An Emerging Understanding of the Reflective (Meta) Experience of Mood, unpublished manuscript (1993), https://ohsu.pure.elsevier.com/en/publications

111. *Ibid*

112. *Ibid* at 48.

113. Daniel Goleman, Emotional Intelligence at 46.

114. *Ibid*

115. Olivier Serrat, *Understanding and Developing Emotional Intelligence*, https://link.springer.com/chapter/10.1007/978-981-10-0983-9_37.

116. *Ibid* at 43.

117. *Ibid*

118. *Ibid* at 55.

119. *Ibid* at 49.

120. *Ibid* at 55.

121. In *Wyatt v. Stickney*, Wyatt v. Stickney, 325 F. Supp. 781 (M.D.Ala. 1971). the federal court declared conditions at Bryce intolerable, that improper treatments there were designed only to make the patients more manageable. The resulting court-ordered agreements formed the basis for federal minimum standards for the care of people with mental illness or mental retardations who reside in institutional settings.

122. Olivier Serrat, *Understanding and Developing Emotional Intelligence* https://link.springer.com/chapter/10.1007/978-981-10-0983-9_37.

123. Shales, Janet M., Ph.D., Forgiveness and Emotional Intelligence, August 4, 2017, https://www.linkedin.com/pulse/forgiveness-emotional-intelligence

124. Beverly Flanigan, Forgiving the Unforgivable 5 (Wiley Publishing Inc. 1992).

125. John Hopkins Medicine, https://www.hopkinsmedicine.org/health/wellness-and-prevention/forgiveness-your-health-depends-on-it; J Orathinkal and A Vansteenwegen (2006). The effect of forgiveness on marital satisfaction in relation to marital stability *Contemporary Family Therapy*, 28(2): 251-260 and P Gangdev (2009); *Forgiveness: A Note for Psychiatrists*. 51 (2) INDIAN J. Psychiatry 153-156.

126. *Ibid*

127. *Ibid*

128. Loren Toussaint and Jon R. Webb, "Theoretical and Empirical Connections Between Forgiveness, Mental Health and Well-Being," in *Handbook of Forgiveness*, ed. Everett L. Worthington Jr. (New York" Brunner- Routledge, 2005), pp. 349-362.

129. Everett L. Worthington, Jr., A Just Forgiveness: Responsible Healing without Excusing Injustice 78 (Downers Grove, IL: InterVarsity Press 2009).

130. *Ibid*

131. *Ibid*

132. Anthony Ray Hinton (eji.org)

133. *Ibid*

134. *Ibid* See also Anthony Ray Hinton, The Sun Does Shine St Martins Press 2018.

135. Luke 23:33-34

136. Aristotle, *The Nichomachean Ethics*.

137. Daniel Goleman, *Emotional Intelligence 96* (Bantam Books 1995).

138. *Ibid* at 97

139. Daniel Goleman, Emotional Intelligence: Why It Can Matter More Than IQ 115 (New York: Bloomsbury, 1995); Richard Wiseman, The Luck Factor 37 (Cornerstone 2004).

140. Richard Wiseman, The Luck Factor 37 (Cornerstone 2004).

141. *Ibid*

142. *Ibid*

143. *Ibid* at 106.

144. *Ibid* at 97.

145. Daniel Goleman, *Emotional Intelligence: Why It Can Matter More Than IQ 99*(New York: Bloomsbury, 1995).

146. *Ibid* at 146.

147. Michael Lynch, Managing Director and Manager of External Relations for Project Horseshoe Farm.

148. *Ibid* at 105.

149. Tom Rath, Strengths Finder 2.0 at 18 (Gallup Press 2007). There are multiple paradigms for assessing and understanding our strengths that can be very helpful. One of the most widely used is *Gallup Strength Finder* geared toward the business and professional world. Built upon data gathered from 100,000 interviews, and surveys of 10 million people worldwide, Gallup has developed a 34-strength assessment. https://www.gallup.com/cliftonstrengths/en/252137/home.aspx. There are other reputable assessments also available, *see e.g.*, Martin Seligman, https://www.authentichappiness.sas.upenn.edu/ (VIA Survey of Character Strengths)

150. Tom Rath, Strengths Finder 2.0 at 18 (Gallup Press 2007). There are multiple paradigms for assessing and understanding our strengths that can be very helpful. One of the most widely used is *Gallup Strength Finder* geared toward the business and professional world. Built upon data gathered from 100,000 interviews,

and surveys of 10 million people worldwide, Gallup has developed a 34-strength assessment. https://www.gallup.com/cliftonstrengths/en/252137/home.aspx. There are other reputable assessments also available, *see e.g.,* Martin Seligman, https://www.authentichappiness.sas.upenn.edu/ (VIA Survey of Character Strengths)

151. *Ibid* at 19 (emphasis in original).

152. Mihaly Csikszenthihalyi, Finding Flow 27-28 (Basic Books 1997).

153. *Ibid* at 8.

154. Tom Rath Strengths Finder 2.0 at 18 (Gallup Press 2007).

155. *Ibid*

156. *Ibid* at 23.

157. *Ibid* at 157.

158. John Kabat-Zinn, *Full Catastrophe Living 292* (Double Day 1990).

159. John Claypool, *Tracks of a Fellow Struggler 84* (Insight Press 1974).

160. Daniel Goleman, *Adaptability; A Primer 5* (More than Sound, LLC 2017).

161. *Ibid*

162. *Ibid*

163. *Ibid*

164. Fewell, Danna Nolan & David Miller GUNN, *COMPROMISING Redemption — Relating Characters in the Book of ruth* (Westminster/John Knox Press, Louisville, Kentucky 1999). *See also* Genesis 10; Deuteronomy 23: 2-4

165. *Ibid*

166. Ronald A. Simkins, Thomas M. Kelly, J. eds, The Bible, the Economy and the Poor, Religion and Society (2014); http://moses.creighton.edu/JRs/2014/2014-11.pdf

167. Joan D. Chittister, *The Story of Ruth: Twelve Moments in Every Woman's Life 61* (William B. Eerdmans Publishing Company 2000).

168. *Ibid* at 88.

169. John Kabat-Zinn, *Full Catastrophe Living 292* (Double Day 1990).

170. John Kabat-Zinn, *Full Catastrophe Living 292* (Double Day 1990).

171. Guy Winch, *Emotional First Aid: Practical Strategies for Treating Failure, Rejection, Guilt and Other Everyday Psychological Injuries* (Hudson Street Press 2012).

172. John Kabat-Zinn, *Full Catastrophe Living 169* (Double Day 1990).

173. *Ibid*

174. Steven M. Southwick, M.D. and Dennis S. Charney, M.D., *Resilience: The Science of Mastering Life's Greatest Challenges 172* (Cambridge University Press 2015).

175. John Claypool, *Mending the Heart xiv* (Browman & Littlefield 1999).

176. In 1992, Gene Stallings, the head football coach at the University of Alabama, and his wife helped expand the RISE Center, where their son, Johnny, who had Down Syndrome, had attended. The Stallings Center at RISE serves as a national model for similar programs throughout the United States. It has six classrooms, serves 80 children, and has 34 staff including, a speech therapist, a physical therapist, and an occupational therapist. The RISE Center hosts 12,000 visitors each year and serves as a practicum and internship for 80 University of Alabama students each year. https://risecenter.ua.edu/about.html

177. https://btaylor.people.ua.edu

178. Joan D. Chittister, *The Story of Ruth: Twelve Moments in Every Woman's Life 67* (Wm. B. Eerdmans Publishing Co. 2000).

179. *Ibid* at 25, 61.

180. Joan D. Chittister, *The Story of Ruth: Twelve Moments in Every Woman's Life* 1,3 (William B. Eerdmans Publishing Company 2000).

181. https://www.gotquestions.org/meaning-of-hesed.html

182. Matthew 1:1-16.

183. 1 Thessalonians 5:16

184. Chemosh, a god who demanded child sacrifice.

185. Phyllis Trible, *Ruth, Jewish Women's Archive*, https://jwa.org/encyclopedia/article/ruth-bible

186. Joan D. Chittister, *The Story of Ruth: Twelve Moments in Every Woman's Life* 1,3 (William B. Eerdmans Publishing Company 2000) (quote does not show ellipsis).

187. Martin Seligman, *Authentic Happiness* 78 (Free Press 2002).

188. Erin C McCanlies, Ja Kook Gu, Michael E Andrew, John M Violanti, *The Effect of Social Support, Gratitude, Resilience and Satisfaction with Life on Depressive Symptoms Among Police Officers Following Hurricane Katrina*, Int J Soc Psychiatry 64:63- 72 (2018); Emmons and McCullough, *Counting Blessings Versus Burdens" An Experimental Investigation of Gratitude and Subjective Well-Being in Daily Life*, 84 J. of Personality and Social Psychology 377–389 (2003). A. Killen, A. Macaskill, *Using a Gratitude Intervention to Enhance Well-Being in Older Adults*, J. Happiness Studies (2015). See also Linda Roszak Burton, Gratitude Heals: A Journal for Inspiration and Guidance (Publishing Partner 2019).

189. McCraty & Childre, *The Grateful Heart: The Psychophysiology of Appreciation* cited in R. A. Emmons & M. E. McCullough (Eds.), *The psychology of gratitude* 230–255 (Oxford University Press 2004); Emily Fletcher, *The Neuroscience of Gratitude*, HuffPost Dec. 6. 2017.

190. Roland Zahn, Jorge Moll, Mirella Paiva, Griselda Garrido, Frank Krueger, Edward D. Huey, and Jordan Grafman *The Neural Basis of Human Social Values: Evidence from Functional MRI*, 19 Cereb Cortex. 276-283 (Feb 2009),Published online 2008 May 22. doi: 10.1093/cercor/bhn080'; McCraty & Childre, *The Grateful Heart: The Psychophysiology of Appreciation* cited in R. A. Emmons & M. E. McCullough (Eds.), *The psychology*

of gratitude 230–255 (Oxford University Press 2004); Emily Fletcher, *The Neuroscience of Gratitude*, HuffPost Dec. 6. 2017.

191. Alex Korb, *The Grateful Brain*, Psychology Today (Nov 20, 2012) https://www.psychologytoday.com/us/blog/prefrontal-nudity/201211/the-grateful-brain

192. Martin Seligman, *Authentic Happiness 40-43* (Free Press 2002).

193. Daniel Goleman, *Emotional Intelligence: Why it Can Matter More Than IQ 169* (Bloomsbury 1996).

194. *Ibid* at 171.

195. *Ibid* at 172.

196. *Ibid* at 170-172.

197. "Any kind of expectation creates a problem. We should accept, but not expect. Whatever comes, accept it, whatever goes, accept it. The immediate benefit is that your mind is always peaceful." Sri Swami Satchidanandea.

198. "Is there life after death? a disciple once asked a Holy One. And the Holy answered, "The great spiritual question is not, Is there life after death? The great spiritual question is, Is there life before death?" Joan Chittister, Rule of Benedict: Insights for the Ages, A Spirituality for the 21st Century (Spiritual Legacy Series 2010).

199. "I no longer want to have anything to do with love that forgets to be grateful." Thomas Merton, The Sign of Jonas 290.

200. Joan Chittister, Rule of Benedict: Insights for the Ages, A Spirituality for the 21st Century (Spiritual Legacy Series 2010).

201. Elosua, Maria, *The Influence of Gratitude in Physical, Psychological, and Spiritual Well-Being.* 17 Journal of Spirituality in Mental Health. 110-118. (2015) *citing* Carman & Streng, 1989.

202. There are five key elements of emotional intelligence: Self-awareness, Self-regulation, Motivation, Empathy, Social skills. Daniel Goleman, Emotional Intelligence: Why It Can Matter More Than IQ 172 (New York: Bloomsbury, 1995).

203. Martin Seligman and Chris Peterson, *Character Strengths and Virtues* (Oxford University Press 2004).

204. Steven M. Southwick, M.D. and Dennis S. Charney, M.D., *Resilience: The Science of Mastering Life's Greatest CHALLENGES* (Cambridge University Press 2015).

205. https://museumandmemorial.eji.org/museum

www.ingramcontent.com/pod-product-compliance
Lightning Source LLC
Chambersburg PA
CBHW032258150426
43195CB00008BA/501